BRISTOL 408

JAMES NICHOLLS

AMBERLEY

Front cover: Bristol 408-1-001. (James Nicholls)
Back cover: Bristol 408-1-001. (James Nicholls)

First published 2023

Amberley Publishing
The Hill, Stroud,
Gloucestershire, GL5 4EP

www.amberley-books.com

ISBN: 978 1 3981 1618 4 (print)
ISBN: 978 1 3981 1619 1 (ebook)

British Library Cataloguing in Publication Data.
A catalogue record for this book is available from the British Library.

Typeset in 10pt on 13pt Celeste.
Typesetting by SJmagic DESIGN SERVICES, India.
Printed in the UK.

Contents

1

The Background

Bristol Cars has a long and distinguished history dating back to the mid-nineteenth century. Indeed, the eponymous name dates back virtually to the time when the city of Bristol itself was a hub for the Industrial Revolution and of the British Empire. Bristol, a home for pirates, privateers and, unfortunately, the brutal slave trade from Africa and the West Indies, became an incredibly wealthy city and Great Britain's largest maritime port after London. Through the innovative thinking of its famous sons such as Isambard Kingdom Brunel, Bristol became one of the leading and most modern cities imaginable.

Engineer Brunel (1806–59), designer of many bridges, tunnels, railway lines and ships, is perhaps most well known for the steam ships *Great Western* (1837) and the stupendous *Great Britain* (1857) the world's first iron-hulled, steam-powered, propeller-driven passenger liner, the Great Western Railway from Bristol to the capital, the Clifton Suspension Bridge, completed in 1864, and the docks at Bristol. Due to the enormous tidal range of the River Avon, docking in Bristol had always been a risky business for cargo ships. These ships would rest on the bed of the river when the tide went out, causing immense pressure on the hulls. Wooden ships built in Bristol were very well made and withstood this pressure, leading to the saying, 'shipshape and Bristol fashion'. Brunel was one of the exponents of the floating harbour created in the city centre utilising a lock system and allowing ships to stay afloat whatever the state of the tide.

Another of the great industrialist designers of the nineteenth century, influenced by and following in the footsteps of inventors like Brunel, was George White. White, the founder of Bristol Cars, was born amid this melting pot of technological and scientific advancement and social change in 1856. A precocious talent, by the age of sixteen, White had established himself as the company secretary of the Bristol Tramways Company. He moved up through the organisation to become the managing director for this new mode of transport. The tram was originally a horse-drawn form of transport from a to b and unsuited to the hilly streets of Bristol with the very steep Park Street at its centre. White therefore struck upon the idea to solve this problem with the development of 'electric street traction' and conceived the infrastructure of an integrated network linking the whole of the dynamic city of Bristol including rail, tram, bus, train stations, city centre and suburbs. His revolutionary new method of transportation was adopted in other neighbouring towns and cities including Bath, Cheltenham, Gloucester, Swindon, Wells and even London. Everyone from all walks of life benefited from the convenience, speed and affordability of this new and previously unheard of 'public transport'. Mobility and travel were no longer the preserve of the wealthy few.

White also developed a new company, the Bristol Commercial Vehicles Division, which designed and built a more efficient and capable bus service than anything that had been seen before. The Bristol C40 bus was launched in 1908 and proved itself more powerful and faster than any competitor. In that same year White drove another nail into the coffin of the horse-drawn era with the launch of his 'Blue Taxi' service of petrol-powered cabs.

By 1911 George White's visionary company was manufacturing trams, buses and coaches, vans and lorries, hearses and taxis, which were being exported around the globe, with Bristol vehicles in service in the USA, Australia and much of Europe. At the same time White and his sons were also alert to new developing forms of transport, most notably the motor car and of course the idea of the aeroplane. It was George White who masterminded and developed the commercial use of the aeroplane in Britain.

Less than seven years after the Wright brothers first manned flight of the length of just a football field, in 1910 Sir George, as he was now known, having been made a baronet in 1904, and his sons Samuel and Stanley founded the British and Colonial Aeroplane Company, the world's first commercial aeroplane company. In that same year the first Bristol Boxkite plane flew and landed safely at Filton, just 5 or 6 miles north of Bristol. A year later the company was the largest manufacturer of aircraft in the world. The speed of development, innovation and sophistication was extreme, and with the outbreak of the First World War became exponential. The Bristol Scout, which was launched just prior to the outbreak of hostilities, was highly manoeuvrable and capable of attaining nearly 100 mph. The fledgling aeroplane company received a huge order of over 400 units for what would become known as the fast and manoeuvrable *Bristol Bullet*.

At the end of the war the company was restructured and renamed the Bristol Aeroplane Company, and still under the auspices of the White family continued to grow to the extent that by 1929 more than half of the world's aircraft were powered by Bristol Aero engines. The company tagline was 'Dependability and Power' – this was no mere solipsism as proven by the fact the between 1929 and 1937 the world altitude record was broken five times utilising Bristol Aero engines. As Britain entered into the Second World War in late 1939, both the Bristol Aero Company and Bristol Commercial Vehicles would once again play an enormous part in the war effort. The aero engine division alone produced over 100,000 units during this time and many famous names were immortalised including the Blenheim, the Beaufighter, and the Hercules engine, the 1,735 hp 'whispering giant' of which 57,400 units were built. Even so, research and development still continued apace with jet engine and helicopter divisions established, and in 1947 the Bristol Sycamore helicopter was launched, the design of which remained in use for several decades.

Bristol, the iconic bespoke car manufacturer, took its name from the Bristol Aeroplane Company, which formed a car division in 1945. A small factory was established at the Filton Aerodrome, where the company had its headquarters and where the cars were made. It was intended from the beginning that the cars should be built in small numbers and to the very highest standards, in order to exploit the skills of the designers, inspectors and craftsmen who were recruited from the airframe and engines divisions of the company.

This was an ideal way in which to utilise the experience and technical expertise garnered by the workforce during wartime and, quite importantly, keep some of these 50,000 workers employed now that there were no more military contracts to otherwise occupy them.

War is a dirty business and it would seem that Bristol gained some significant advantages by obtaining the rights to the defeated German BMW 327 chassis and highly successful 328 2-litre racing engine through wartime reparation. Initially working with AFN, the company which had been selling Frazer Nash-BMWs before the war, the first cars were designated Frazer-Nash-Bristol, but in 1947 the first Bristol proper, the 400, was launched using lightweight aluminium construction and stringent aircraft standards, and in 1948 it was driven by Freddie March, 9th Duke of Richmond, around Goodwood Motor Circuit for its official opening. The 400 only had a 2-litre engine but due to its use of aluminium, beneficial aerodynamics, and aircraft build quality it was very reliable and capable of 104 mph (166 km/h), making it very popular among the motorsport fraternity.

Bristols were lightweight, streamlined from wind-tunnel testing and constructed to the highest standards, creating a car that was reliable, comfortable and offered good performance. The Bristol 400 and its successor the 401 had class successes in the 1948 Mille Miglia, and Tulip and Alpine Rallies. The excellent Bristol engine, developed from the BMW, was incredibly sought after and many of the great racing cars of the 1950s were powered by it: Arnolt-Bristol, Cooper Bristol, AC, ERA, Frazer Nash, Bristol-Lister, Tojeiro-Bristol, Bristol-Lotus. Meanwhile the Bristol 450 took all three podium spots in

FOREWORD

The announcement, in recent months, that The Bristol Aeroplane Company Ltd., and A.F.N. Ltd. (manufacturers of Frazer-Nash cars) were to combine forces with, as their aim, the production of high-performance cars, undoubtedly created very considerable interest, both in this country and overseas.

Excellent progress has been achieved and it is now possible to announce provisional details of the specification. Whilst these will serve to create a general picture of the post-war Frazer-Nash, it is not possible, within the limits of this leaflet, adequately to convey to the prospective owner the high standard of design and construction to which these cars will be built, although this may perhaps be expected as a natural result of the outstanding technical knowledge of The Bristol Aeroplane Company in aircraft and aero-engine design, combined with the long and successful experience and world-wide reputation behind Frazer-Nash cars.

A comprehensive catalogue with illustrations of the various models and prices, will be issued in due course.

Technical perfection in design combined with superlative behaviour on the road, distinctive appearance and luxury of equipment.

Frazer-Nash-Bristol. The foreword from the brochure announcing the new car company. (James Nicholls)

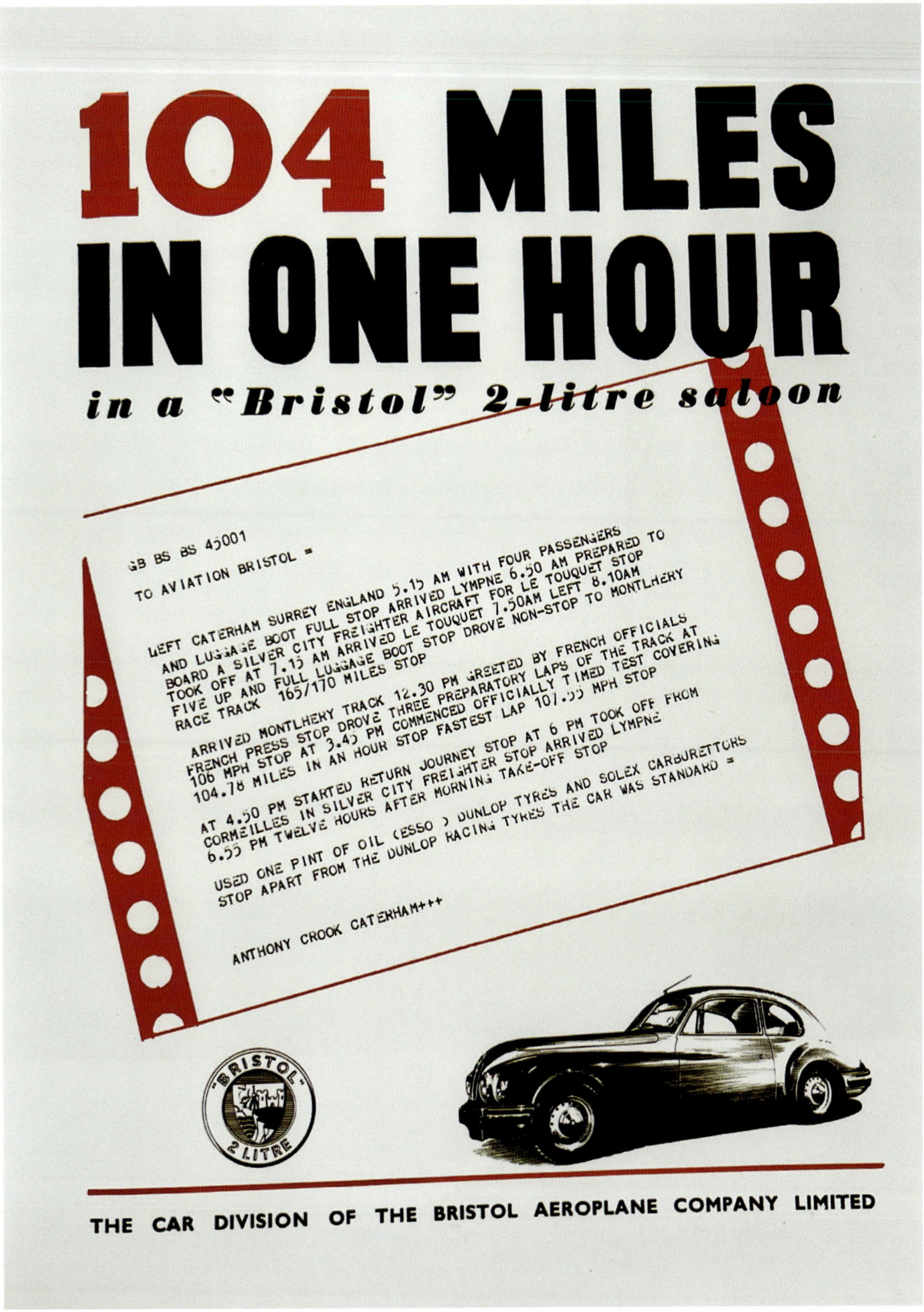

An early advertisement extolling the virtues of the Bristol 400. (James Nicholls)

1955 Arnolt-Bristol Competition model. The July 1956 issue *of Sport Car Illustrated* magazine said, 'In terms of performance, the Arnolt-Bristol is a thoroughbred racing car fit to be stabled with Ferraris and Mercedes. Its acceleration is shattering.' (*Benzina* magazine)

Bristol-engined racing cars at the 2016 Goodwood Revival. (James Nicholls)

Close-up of the magnificent Bristol engine installed in a 1956 AC Aceca. (James Nicholls)

its class in both 1954 and 1955 (and seventh, eighth, and ninth overall that year) at the Le Mans 24 Hour Race, where one of the cars recorded 150.34 mph (240.544 km/h) on the Mulsanne straight. Right through the 1950s Bristol cars were essentially built and developed in the rarified atmosphere of the aeroplane factory and benefitted from the associated technology, which led to the production of some of the most sophisticated and sought-after cars capable of prodigious mileage and longevity combined with comfort and speed. Cars such as the convertible 402, known as the 'Hollywood Express' after actors Jean Simmons and her husband Stewart Granger purchased two of the just twenty-one units built, while Sir Tom Barr Smith and his brother, of Adelaide, also purchased a pair. Both Australian cars remain in Australia with Sir Tom's now owned by his son Tom. Many consider Bristol's apotheosis of its early cars to be the 'Gentleman's Express', the 404 of which *Autosport* magazine's writer John Bolster said in his road test of 16 October 1953, 'The Bristol is an expensive car, but it gives that indefinable feeling of quality that only big money can buy. The upholstery and interior trim, the walnut dashboard with its array of accurate instruments, the excellent finish of every little detail – all these things make this vehicle worth its price to the man who must have the best ... For a long fast journey à deux, the 404 is a magic carpet indeed.'

The 406, another fast two-door sports touring saloon with its legendary 2-litre engine now increased to 2.2 litres, was made even more beautiful with stunning interpretations by Carrozzeria Zagato of Milan, which also produced the Aston Martin DB4 GT. Both were shown together at the 1959 London Motor Show at Earls Court. The Bristol 406 Zagato that

The 1950 Bristol 402, the convertible car nicknamed the Hollywood Express due to a pair being purchased by actors Stewart Granger and Jean Simmons. (Courtesy of the owner)

One of two Bristol 402 cars being unloaded upon arrival in Australia. (Courtesy of the owner)

1954 Bristol 404. Lighter and now without the BMW-look grille, the 404 had an 18-inch shorter wheelbase than its predecessor. John Bolster of *Autosport* magazine called it 'a magic carpet indeed'. (Courtesy of the owner)

1961 Aston Martin DB4 GT Zagato at Villa Erba, Lake Como, Italy. A rare and astronomically expensive motor car today. (James Nicholls)

1959 Bristol 406 Zagato. Number one of just six built by Zagato of Milan to the requirements of Anthony Crook. Lighter and smaller than the standard 406 saloon. (James Nicholls)

Detail of the 1959 Bristol 406 by Zagato. (James Nicholls)

was on show in London, the first of just six cars produced, of which only five are extant, now resides in Melbourne, Australia.

The 1960s saw a change in direction for Bristol with the traditional and much trusted six-cylinder engine utilised up until it was replaced with a V8 engine! In order to compete with the top end speed of other luxury cars such as Facel Vega, Jaguar and Aston Martin, the current engine could be developed no further. For example, in 1959/60 the 406 was capable of only 163 km/h but was more expensive than a Jaguar XK 150 3.8 S, Facel Vega HK 500, Lancia Flaminia Sport Zagato, all of which were much faster, and even more expensive than an Aston Martin DB4, which had a top end speed of over 50 km/h more. So, while the 407, launched in 1961, resembled its predecessor the 406 in looks, with the new special order and modified Canadian-built 5,130 cc Chrysler engine and Torque-flite automatic transmission, it was now capable of a maximum speed of 122 mph (195 km/h), up from 102 mph (163 km/h), and could go from 0–60 mph in under ten seconds, 2.6 seconds quicker than the 406. The aluminium-bodied, two-door 407 saloon was incredibly powerful and amazingly cosseting for its passengers and set the standard for Bristol cars well into the 1970s, before another complete change of style with the introduction of the 412 penned

A 1962 Facel Vega Facel II at the Concorso d'Eleganza Villa d'Este. Facel Vega was one of the other manufacturers using a big American engine as was Bristol. (James Nicholls)

Overall Length........................199 inches   Overall Height (Unladen)...........60 inches
Overall Width.......................... 68 inches   Ground Clearance (Unladen)...... 6½ inches
Kerb Weight...............3584 lbs

Bristol Type 407 Car

iii

The Bristol 407 as depicted in the Bristol Workshop Manual Type 407 and 408 (up to chassis number 408/7200). (James Nicholls)

by Zagato in 1975, a design reminiscent of the Lancia Beta Spider from the same house. A. G. Pritchard in *The Sporting Motorist* October 1962 wrote, 'Production of Bristol cars continues, but inevitably rising costs and competition from mass-production rivals are increasingly difficult to combat. The place of such cars on the motoring scene is somewhat problematical, but for sheer quality they are without equal.'

2

The Bristol V8 Motor Cars

The vehicle that Bristol produced in 1963 was its finest to date. Some may argue that the Bristol 408 was the zenith of the marque's output and that what came after was rather like the fall of the Roman Empire with an ever-increasing succession of more powerful, bloated and vulgar iterations of the previous model leading to a decline and fall at the hands of outsiders while those in power 'fiddled while Rome burned'.

Original handbooks for the Bristol Type 407 car. (James Nicholls)

Overall Length .... 193½ inches
Overall Width .... 68 inches
Overall Height (Unladen) .... 59 inches
Ground Clearance (Unladen) .... 6½ inches
Kerb Weight .... 3528 lb.

Bristol Type 408 Mk.1 Car

V

The Bristol 408 as depicted in the Bristol Workshop Manual Type 407 and 408 (up to chassis number 408/7200). The car shown is chassis number 408/7001. (James Nicholls)

The 408, however, was a magnificent motor car and one of the very best that Bristol, one of the finest of all manufacturers, ever produced in its chequered history between 1947 and its final demise in 2020. Mechanically very similar to its predecessor the 407, the Bristol 408 introduced Armstrong Select-a-ride damping and was, otherwise, a visual update of the 407 but with a wider rectangular grille opening and headlights mounted on flat panels, with a slightly flatter roof and bonnet. This is the second Bristol model to feature the modified Canadian-built Chrysler V8s, with the 408 having a slightly increased engine capacity to 5.2 litres.

Bristol Cars Ltd launched the 5-litre Type 408 Saloon at the 48th International Motor Exhibition, on stand number 94 on the ground floor of the Earls Court Motor Show on the 16–26 October 1963. In purely factual terms the car can be described, as Bristol did in the official catalogue (priced at two shillings and sixpence), as follows. Engine: 8-cylinder, 90 degree Vee, bore 98.5 mm, stroke 84.07 mm, capacity 5,130 cc, developing 250 bhp. at 4,400 rpm, maximum torque 340 lb/ft at 2,800 rpm., compression ratio 9:1, overhead valves, push-rod operated; Carter 4-choke downdraught carburettor with extra large air filter/silencer; automatic choke for cold starting; manifold heat control for rapid warm up; mechanical fuel pump; cooling pressurised, centrifugal water pump circulation thermostatically controlled; twin electric fans operated by thermostat control; temperature gauge on instrument panel; rotor-type oil pump; by-pass oil filter; pressure gauge on

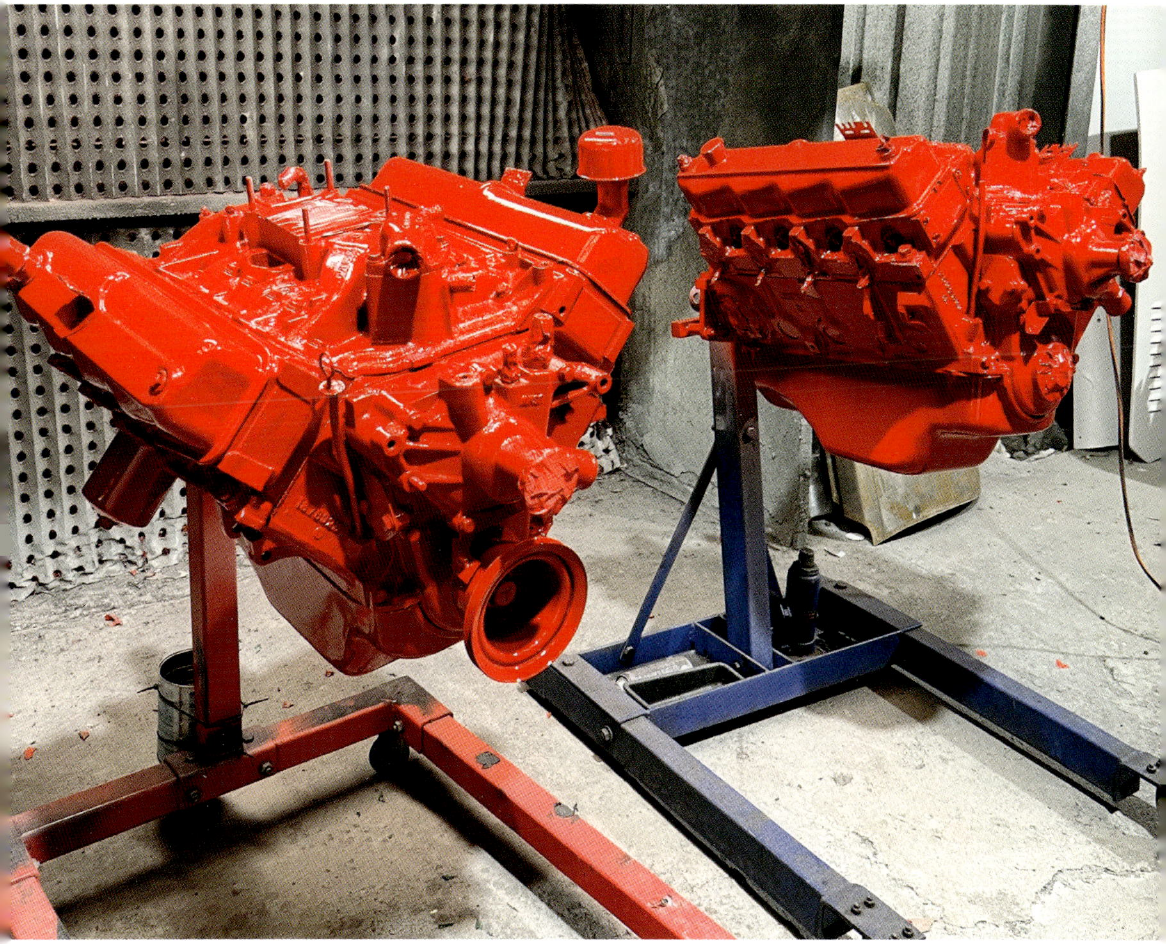

Two big red lumps, as L. J. K. Setright termed the V8 Chrysler engine for the Bristol. On the left for the Type 408 and on the right for a Type 410. (Justin Hills)

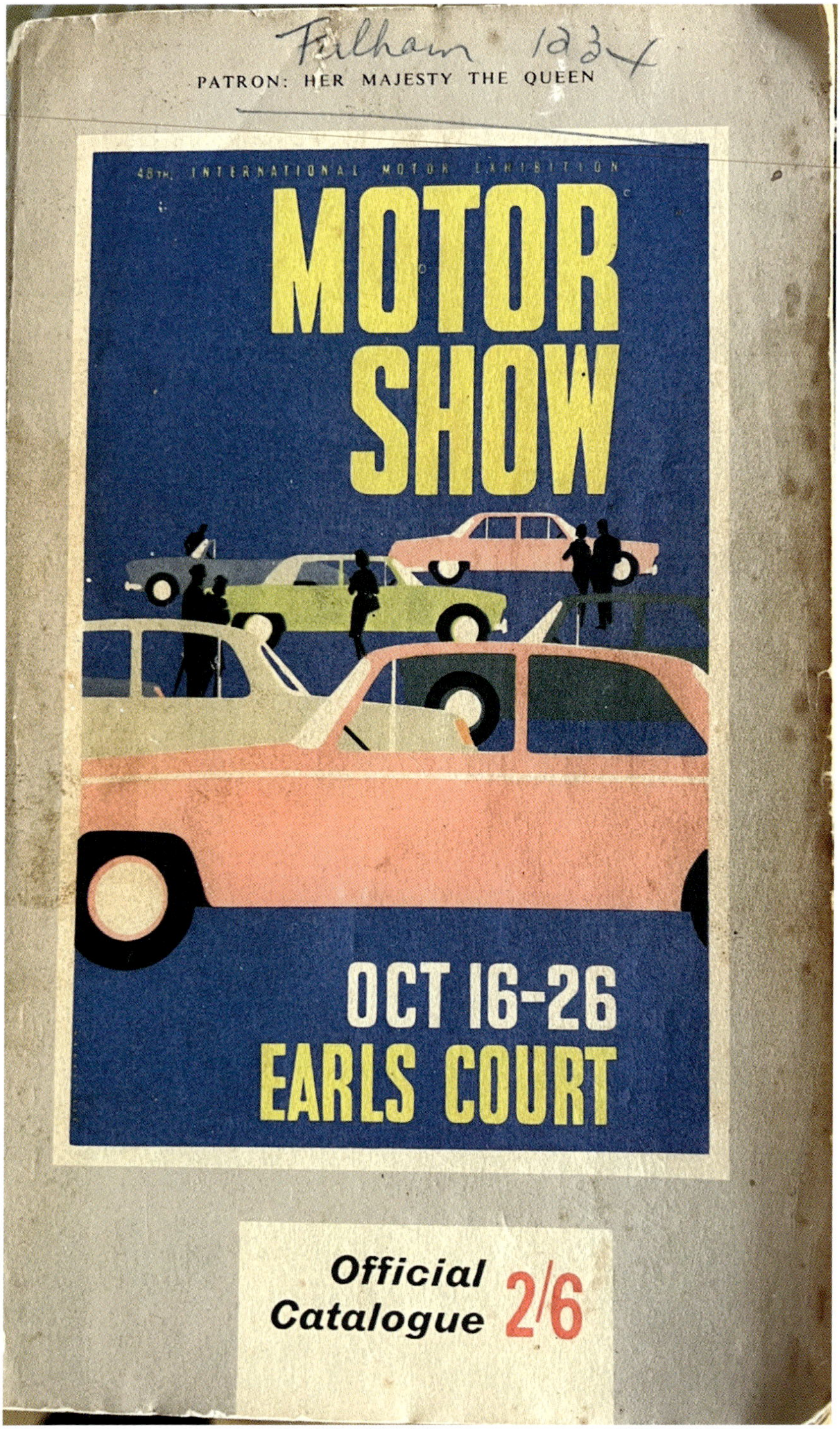

The cover of the official catalogue for 48th International Motor Exhibition Motor Show held at Earls Court, London, on 16–26 October 1963. Bristol Cars Ltd of Filton, Bristol, appeared on page 115. (James Nicholls)

instrument panel; 12-volt electrical system positive-earth ignition system; centrifugally and vacuum controlled advance and retard; 72 amp/hr battery; ventilated dynamo; Torque-flite 3 forward speeds and reverse automatic transmission with fluid torque converter; variable ratio drive; intermediate gear holds, gears selected by push-buttons illuminated on facia panel; ratios low 8.1, intermediate 4.8, high 3.31, reverse 7.28; torque converter stalled ratio 2.2:1; open propeller shaft; hypoid rear axle; Dunlop hydraulic self-adjusting servo-assisted disc brakes on all wheels; disc diameter 11¼ inches; pull up type handbrake mounted on floor between front seats; Marles worm-type steering, 17-inch 2-spoke adjustable steering wheel; front suspension independent by wishbones of unequal length with coiled springs, telescopic hydraulic dampers, torsional anti-roll bar; rear suspension by torsion bars; Watts linkage, electrically adjustable telescopic dampers; Smiths Bevelift jacking system using built-in jacking points; Dunlop pressed steel perforated bolt-on disc wheels, wide base rims; Dunlop R.S.5. 6.00-16 tyres and tubes. Full 4-seater saloon, light alloy body; 2 doors hinged on front pillars; adjustable front seats; backs fully reclining; seats tip forward for easy access to rear seats accommodating 2 persons in comfort, with folding centre armrest; interior upholstered in high quality hide over foam rubber cushions and backs; polished walnut woodwork; foam rubber protection pads above and below facia panel; pile carpet with felt underlays over soundproofed floor; opening rear quarterlights; lockable glove box; pockets in doors, on rear of front seats and at side of rear seats; roof light operated by door opening and switch on facia panel; bonnet lock controlled by interior lever; sun visors; built-in heater system, fresh air at desired volume or temperature, incorporating screen demisting and defrosting, controls on facia panel; instruments grouped in cowl in front of driver, rheostat controlled illumination, including ammeter, electric clock, 4 inch diameter speedometer with trip recorder, 4 inch diameter tachometer, petrol gauge, oil pressure gauge, water temperature gauge, dual 2-speed self-parking windscreen wipers and windscreen washers, warning lights for ignition, head lamp main beam, direction indicators, petrol reserve and brake fluid level; reserve fuel supply operated by solenoid switch. Equipment includes: 4 sealed beam head lamp system; foot dipper switch; lever on steering column operates head lamp flashing switch, also direction indicator switch; side lamps; twin rear lights incorporating red reflectors; twin automatic reversing lights; rear number plate light; luggage boot light; twin windtone horns; driving mirror; 4 ashtrays; cigar lighter; lockable petrol filler; full width front and rear bumpers; spare wheel housed in readily accessible compartment in nearside front wing; a similar compartment containing battery, brake servo and fuse box on offside; luggage boot capacity 19 cu. ft; fuel tank capacity 18 Imp. Gal. including 2 ½ gal. reserve. Wheelbase 9 ft. 6 in., track, front 4 ft. 5 in., rear 4 ft. 6 ½ in.; overall length 16 ft. 1 ½ in., width 5 ft. 8 in., height 4 ft. 11 in.; turning circle 39 ft. 6 in.; ground clearance 6 ½ in.; kerb weight approximately 3,584 lb. Available in single or duotone metallic colours. Provision made for easy fitting of radio as optional extra with twin speakers and balance control. Also available with left-hand steering.

The actual car displayed at Earls Court was the second Bristol 408 to be built, car number 408-1-002, engine number 949-23729C and chassis number 408-7002, and it was presented in metallic silver coachwork with a contrasting black roof. It was awarded the Society of Motor Manufacturers & Traders bodywork prize for a motor car not costing more than £4,000 excluding purchase tax. The price to buy the car in October 1963 was £3,690 plus £769 6*s* 3*d*, making a total of £4,459 6*s* 3*d*. This was a staggering amount of money at the time.

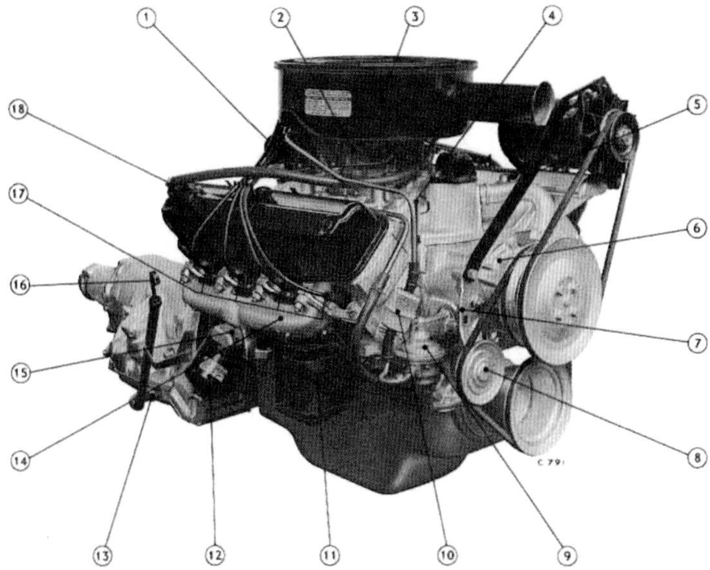

Fig.5 R.H. View of Engine and Transmission

KEY TO FIG. 5

1. Coil.
2. Carburettor.
3. Carburettor Air Cleaner.
4. Engine Dipstick.
5. Generator Belt Adjustment Strap.
6. Water Pump.
7. Idler Pulley Adjustment Bracket.
8. Idler Pulley.
9. Fuel Pump.
10. Fuel Filter.
11. Engine Mounting.
12. Oil Filter.
13. Transmission Drain Plug.
14. Exhaust Manifold.
15. Manifold Heat Control Valve.
16. Transmission Dipstick and Oil Filler Tube.
17. Sparking Plugs and Leads.
18. Smog Pack.

-6-

A labelled right-hand view of the Chrysler engine used in the Bristol Type 408 taken from the Bristol Workshop Manual. (James Nicholls)

Right: A labelled left-hand view of the Chrysler engine used in the Bristol Type 408 taken from the Bristol Workshop Manual. (James Nicholls)

Below: The Bristol Type 408 that appeared on the Bristol stand at the Earls Court Motor Show in 1963. Chassis number 7002.

Fig.6 L.H. View of Engine and Transmission

KEY TO FIG. 6

1. Generator.
2. Oil Filler Pipe Cap Air Cleaner.
3. Distributor.
4. Sparking Plugs and Leads.
5. Transmission Unit.
6. Exhaust Manifold.
7. Starter Motor.
8. Engine Mounting.
9. Oil Pan (Sump).

-7-

A Jensen CV8 photographed at Sydney Olympic Park. (James Nicholls)

A detail of the 1964 Aston Martin DB5 with Touring of Milan Superleggera bodywork used in the James Bond films. (James Nicholls)

Above: The Bristol Type 408 was more expensive at the time than the AC Cobra – not today! (James Nicholls)

Right: The author standing next to the 1961 Jaguar E-Type Series 1 roadster, which he had previously owned. (Jack Severino Nicholls)

To put it in perspective and to show what a good motor car the hand-built Bristol was, it was more expensive than every other car you could buy in England except for a Bentley S3, Facel Vega II, Ferrari, Maserati 3500, or Rolls-Royce. It cost more than a Porsche, than a Jensen CV8, an Alvis or even an Aston Martin DB5, which was priced at £4,175 *7s 1d*, though a DB5 Convertible did cost £30 extra, while a Lagonda Rapide was £133 more at £4,592 against the Bristol at £4,459. An AC 'Shelby Cobra' would have cost you only £2,453 in total, while that icons of the Swinging Sixties, the Mini, was under £500 and an E-Type Jaguar only £1,913! For the same price as an E-Type one could also purchase a Riva Ariston motor boat, though the top of the range from the builder of Italian boats synonymous with La Dolce Vita, the Riva Super Tritone, was indeed Bristol money. Lest one might think that you were only paying for luxury, the 408 was no slouch and could hold a Ferrari 250 GT 2+2 over a standing half mile, as confirmed by the December 1964 issue of *Cars Illustrated* magazine: 'Although born of a fairly long line of cars whose appeal is in the connoisseur class, the Bristol 408 is comparatively unknown. In quality of manufacture, it bears comparison with the best products of other British manufacturers of luxury cars, while in performance it is surely sufficient to remark that it will hold a 250 GT 2+2 Ferrari over a standing half-mile'.

The embodiment of la dolce vita in marine form. A Rive Tritone cost approximately the same as a Bristol Type 408 in period. (RM Sotheby's)

The Bristol Type 408 was reportedly faster than a Ferrari 250 GTE. (James Nicholls)

3

Anthony Crook

The idea of putting a big North American power unit into a European motor car was not a new one. The Jensen CV8, Facel Vega HK 500 and the Facel II, Bizzarini 5300 GT, Iso Rivolta, were all powered by American muscle, as were other cars later in the 1960s such as the Jensen Interceptor, De Tomaso Mangusta, AC 428, and the Monteverdi High Speed (along with the Ferrari 500 Superfast, surely the most evocative name ever given to an automobile). By 1960 Bristol Cars Limited was now a private limited company and had

This Bizzarrini photographed at the Concorso d'Eleganza Villa d'Este in 2019 was also driven by American muscle. (James Nicholls)

Another beautiful European car powered by an American V8 engine. The gorgeous Monteverdi High Speed from Switzerland. (James Nicholls)

been sold by what had become Bristol Siddeley Engines Limited (under pressure from the British Government to concentrate on the production of aero engines) to George White (60 per cent) and Anthony Crook (40 per cent). The Bristol Aeroplane Company had merged with Hawker-Siddeley, meaning that Armstrong-Siddeley cars became part of the group. Plans were afoot to take Bristol mass market with cheaper models manufactured in larger numbers. Sir George White, the grandson of Bristol's founding father George White, and Tony Crook, Bristol's distributor in London, had other ideas, however. Without the support of the larger manufacturing group, it was not financially possible to design the requisite bigger and more powerful engine needed to replace the outmoded six-cylinder in-house Bristol engine, and so out of necessity the new owners turned to the Chrysler manufacturing plant in Windsor, Ontario, Canada, for the new Chrysler V8 and attached Torqueflite transmission for a ready-made solution.

White and the incredibly energetic Crook would take Bristol Cars even more upmarket, concentrating on a new style of limited number hand-built cars creating a luxurious, spacious, and powerful grand tourer, more than doubling its engine size from 2,216 cc to 5,130 cc! Crook was very much the driving force behind Bristol Cars Limited, particularly after Sir George White Bt.II suffered a serious accident in 1969 when at the wheel of his stationary Bristol 410 he was hit by a skidding lorry and seriously injured, and thus in 1973 Crook became the sole owner of the company.

The Frazer Nash driven by Tony Crook at the Monaco GP appearing at the 2022 Monaco Grand Prix Historique. (James Nicholls)

Born in 1920 in Manchester, Crook, in a nice coincidence, went to school at Clifton College in Bristol. He was wealthy through the proceeds of his family's coal business and had a taste for fast cars as a young man. According to his obituary in *Motor Sport* magazine in April 2014, he even had an MG PA while still at school, and as a young Flight-Lieutenant during the Second World War owned both of the Alfa Romeo 8C 2900 short chassis cars in the country, including the 1938 Mille Miglia winning car of Sardinian ace Clemente Biondetti, who was ultimately the winner of more Mille Miglie than any other driver. A keen racer, in a BMW 328 Crook won the first post-war meeting in Britain, which had been organised by the Cambridge University Automobile Club at Gransden Lodge, beating the likes of Roy Salvadori, Reg Parnell, and Alec Issigonis, later of Mini fame. Crook had an early affinity with the Bristol straight six-cylinder engine racing in Frazer Nash and Cooper-Bristols. In 1951 he finished in second place to the legendary and subsequent F1 World Champion Mike Hawthorn in the Goodwood racing season. In 1952 he competed in the British Grand Prix and at the non-championship GP in Monaco, the Prix de Monte-Carlo, where he finished in third place in his Frazer Nash Le Mans Replica Mk2. He drove a Cooper Bristol at the 1953 British GP but did not finish due to a broken

The Frazer Nash in which Tony Crook finished third in Monaco, seen here at the 2022 Monaco Grand Prix Hsitorique. (James Nicholls)

fuel line. In all, Crook finished on the victory podium 370 times between 1946 and 1955 before retiring from racing that year after being hit by Stirling Moss in a Porsche Spyder in the dark during the Goodwood Nine Hours, and having to stay in hospital for a fortnight with his injuries. From then on, he concentrated his efforts on his car dealership in Surrey, specialising in the Bristol marque, and then in 1962 opened the splendid and singular Bristol showroom at Nos 368–370 Kensington High Street in London.

Tony Crook was certainly one of those larger-than-life characters of a peculiarly British nature who received part of their education courtesy of their fortune in surviving the Second World War. There were many stories as to his determination and humour, some no doubt apocryphal as when disguised as a wealthy emir he had his fictitious order taken by a famous rival British luxury car brand salesman at a motor show, or on another occasion at a motoring event sporting a name badge with 'A. Crook' upon it. Not one to suffer fools gladly, he eschewed 'gimmicks' such as marketing and advertising, believing that the cars would sell themselves to those who were discerning enough to appreciate them. A true old school gentleman through and through, he sold 50 per cent of Bristol in the late '90s and the remaining half in 2002, though still remaining as managing director of the company until 2007. In 2011 Bristol Cars was placed into administration. An icon of the British motoring industry, indeed of Britain itself, was no more – just another indication of the former

The one and only Bristol Bullet, the last in the line of Bristol motor cars. (Bristol Cars Ltd)

power's decline into mediocrity. The same company responsible for the development of one of the miracles of twentieth century science, the supersonic passenger airliner Concorde, could no longer even build a motor car. Crook passed away on the 21 January 2014 just three weeks before his birthday, aged ninety-three. And yet, in the same way that Britain has reinvented itself, out of the ashes of despondency a new phoenix arose. Bristol, now owned by Frazer-Nash Research (another company in the automotive sphere to have had its peaks and troughs over the years), previewed its first new model at Salon Privé at Blenheim Palace in September 2016, ready for production to begin in 2017 and mark the 70th anniversary of Bristol Cars. The new Bristol Bullet hopefully marked the start of a new era of excellence and would ensure that the Bristol name would live on in the annals of transportation, the car's wings, front grille, and bonnet air-intake providing visual clues to the company's roots as a manufacturer of aeroplanes. It was a false dawn, Bristol finally succumbing once and for all in 2020, the company's chattels sold off ignominiously at auction: in the centenary year of his birth the man who had done so much for Bristol Cars would no doubt have been turning in his grave. As his obituary by Simon Taylor in *Motor Sport* concluded: 'The concept of a gentleman motor manufacturer is now an outdated one, but it described Tony Crook perfectly. Without his uncompromising determination, Bristol would probably not have survived the 1960s; and certainly, it would not have got as far as the 21st century.'

4

408-1-001

Between 1961 and 1963 Bristol built, by hand, just eighty-eight examples of the 407 model. Between 1963 and 1965 it built even less of the 408 model, with only eighty-six constructed by the skilled artisans at Filton – less than one a week. I have already discussed the 408, car number two, but what of car number one, 408-1-001?

Car number 408-1-001, engine number 949-23439C, chassis number 408-7001 had a multiple of uses from new in 1963 when first registered on 6 September that year. It was

The first Bristol Type 408, chassis number 7001. (James Nicholls)

Car number 408-1-001 as it appears on the identification plate of the very first Bristol Type 408. (James Nicholls)

Verification of the engine number 949-23439C of the very first Bristol Type 408. (James Nicholls)

Chassis number 408-7001 on the identification plate of the first Bristol Type 408. (James Nicholls)

owned by Bristol Cars Ltd for the first thirty months of its life and was utilised during that two-and-a-half-year period by Tony Crook himself as his daily driver and as a test/mule development car (for the 409 model of 1965–1967), and also used as the press car for journalists of various magazines to test drive. It was finished in a duo-tone metallic colour combination of gunmetal with a silver grey roof with high quality hide upholstery in warm stone of the finest Connolly leather. This was the car that graced the official brochure printed and issued in October 1963 and which would have been distributed to potential clients at the Earls Court Motor Show in that month. That brochure makes note of the car's, 'supreme performance plus individuality' and promotes it as, '...one of the world's few cars of obvious distinction', while interestingly listing the vehicle specifications in English and in French.

The colour schemes that were offered were available in a choice of ten metallic colours and two plain colours in a single or two-tone combination in the following exterior colours on the beaten aluminium panels: red, sable, gunmetal, dark grey, silver grey, Cambridge grey, mint green, dark green, heather; pastel blue, azure blue and midnight blue. In effect it would have been possible to order the car in the colour of one's choice. The interior upholstery was available in blue, mastic (for French haute couture designer Chloé this is termed as a pink toned cream in case you were wondering), elephant grey, black, red, dove grey, warm stone, and blue, all provided by leather tanners and curriers Connolly, established in 1878 by the brothers Samuel and Frederick Connolly, who were early motoring pioneers. Samuel's son, Frederick Ignatius Connolly, was friends

The front cover of the original sales brochure for Bristol 408 5.2 litre – one of the world's few cars of obvious distinction. (James Nicholls)

with Sir William Lyons of Jaguar, and Jaguar, Rolls-Royce, Bentley, Ferrari and Maserati and other top marques all used Connolly leather as well as Bristol. Connolly leather was also used on the aforementioned Concorde, the Cunard liners *Queen Mary* and *Queen Elizabeth*, seating at the Houses of Lords and Commons, and King Edward VII's Coronation carriage.

Nothing was left to chance on the 408, and the company proudly, and quite rightly, described it thus in the brochure:

> The Bristol 408 – latest of a long line of luxury high performance cars – is even lower and sleeker than its predecessors yet still retains more than adequate head and leg room for four people. The doors are wide enough to allow easy access and open well above kerb level. All the seats are shaped to give armchair comfort and are fully reclining in front. The interior is upholstered in the highest quality leather over foam rubber with extensive use of safety padding – all woodwork is of the finest selected

Wappenbury Hall, the home of Sir William Lyons of Jaguar fame. (Tom Shaw)

walnut. The chassis is a massive steel construction which gives the car outstanding – in fact almost unique – protective strength in the event of impact, and the steering wheel is especially designed to avoid injury to the driver. In addition, mountings for seat belts are provided. To give greater security for high speed driving at night, 4 headlamps have been incorporated unobtrusively in the design. The rear suspension is fitted with 'Selectaride' shock absorbers, allowing the driver to choose the ride he prefers, whether driving at 120 miles per hour on a motorway or through a town at walking pace. Light pedal pressure operates the disc brakes on all four wheels – there is positively no fade even after a number of stops at high speed. The power unit is extremely quiet with a delightfully smooth automatic transmission, but press buttons are provided for those who prefer to select their own gears. This outstanding car, with its tremendous acceleration, has a fantastic potential for high average speeds over long distances and yet it is equally at home as a sedate town carriage. The Bristol 408 stands out as one of the few cars of obvious distinction in today's world of mass production.

This car pictured in the brochure was heavily used in the first few months of it coming into existence. According to its Car Service Record Card by 11 October 1963 it had travelled 1,642 miles and was serviced with anti-freeze added to the radiator for the coming winter (a good precaution as the previous winter, the 'Big Freeze', had been the coldest for more than 200 years since 1740), and a fire extinguisher was fitted.

A page from the sales brochure showing details of Bristol 408-1-001. (James Nicholls)

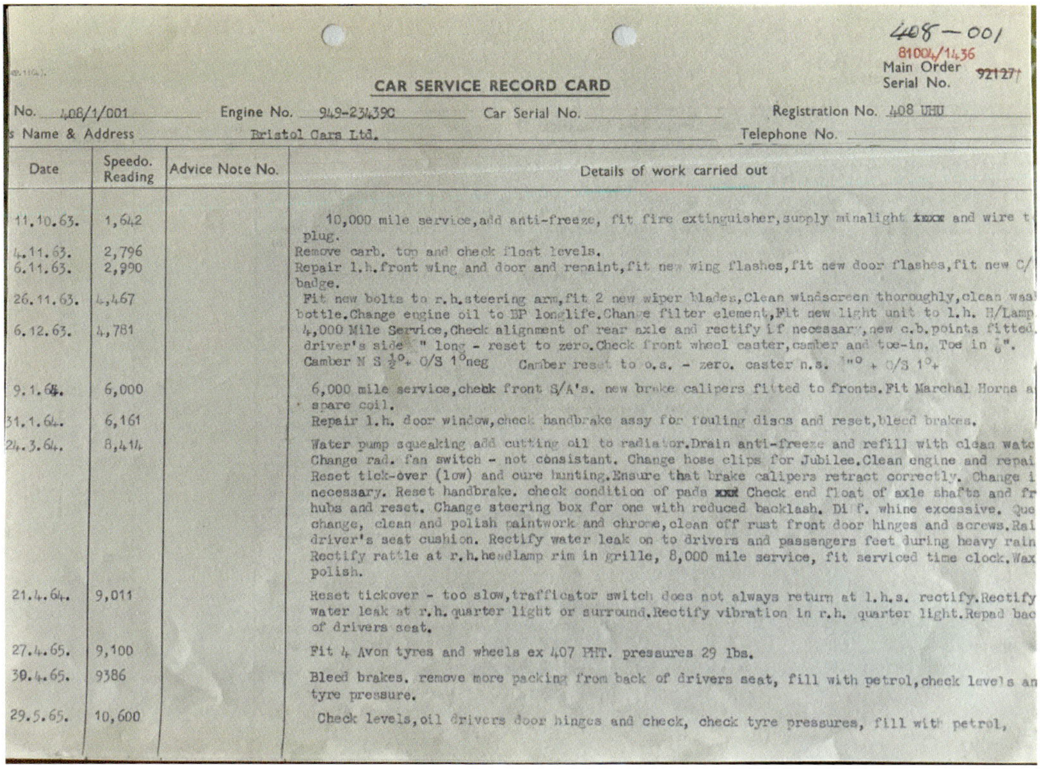

408 – 001

81004/1436

Main Order Serial No. ~~92127~~

CAR SERVICE RECORD CARD

No. 408/1/001 Engine No. 949-23439C Car Serial No. Registration No. 408 UHU

Name & Address Bristol Cars Ltd. Telephone No.

Date	Speedo. Reading	Advice Note No.	Details of work carried out
11.10.63.	1,642		10,000 mile service, add anti-freeze, fit fire extinguisher, supply minalight ~~xxxx~~ and wire t plug.
4.11.63.	2,796		Remove carb. top and check float levels.
6.11.63.	2,990		Repair l.h. front wing and door and repaint, fit new wing flashes, fit new door flashes, fit new C/ badge.
26.11.63.	4,467		Fit new bolts to r.h. steering arm, fit 2 new wiper blades, Clean windscreen thoroughly, clean was bottle. Change engine oil to BP longlife. Change filter element, Fit new light unit to l.h. H/Lamp.
6.12.63.	4,781		4,000 Mile Service, Check alignment of rear axle and rectify if necessary, new c.b. points fitted. driver's side " long - reset to zero. Check front wheel caster, camber and toe-in. Toe in ⅛". Camber N S ½°+ O/S 1°neg Camber reset to o.s. - zero. caster n.s. [illegible]° + O/S 1°+
9.1.64.	6,000		6,000 mile service, check front S/A's. new brake calipers fitted to fronts. Fit Marchal Horns a spare coil.
31.1.64.	6,161		Repair l.h. door window, check handbrake assy for fouling discs and reset, bleed brakes.
24.3.64.	8,414		Water pump squeaking add cutting oil to radiator. Drain anti-freeze and refill with clean wate Change rad. fan switch - not consistant. Change hose clips for Jubilee. Clean engine and repai Reset tick-over (low) and cure hunting. Ensure that brake calipers retract correctly. Change i necessary. Reset handbrake. check condition of pads ~~xxx~~ Check end float of axle shafts and fr hubs and reset. Change steering box for one with reduced backlash. Diff. whine excessive. Que change, clean and polish paintwork and chrome, clean off rust front door hinges and screws. Rai driver's seat cushion. Rectify water leak on to drivers and passengers feet during heavy rain Rectify rattle at r.h. headlamp rim in grille, 8,000 mile service, fit serviced time clock. Wax polish.
21.4.64.	9,011		Reset tickover - too slow, trafficator switch does not always return at l.h.s. rectify. Rectify water leak at r.h. quarter light or surround. Rectify vibration in r.h. quarter light. Repad bac of drivers seat.
27.4.65.	9,100		Fit 4 Avon tyres and wheels ex 407 PHT. pressures 29 lbs.
30.4.65.	9386		Bleed brakes. remove more packing from back of drivers seat, fill with petrol, check levels an tyre pressure.
29.5.65.	10,600		Check levels, oil drivers door hinges and check, check tyre pressures, fill with petrol,

The first page of the Car Service Record card for 408-1-001, owner's name and address showing Bristol Cars Ltd. (James Nicholls)

Just a few weeks later on 4 November 1963, now with 2,796 miles on the speedo, it had its Carter 4-choke carburettor checked. Bonfire night on 5 November obviously caused some fireworks for the following day, having travelled a further 194 miles in forty-eight hours, it came in to the Bristol workshop for repairs – the left-hand front wing and passenger door were repaired and repainted, and new wing and door twin flashes (the *407* featured just a singular chrome strip) and a new Pegasus logo badge by the door fitted. The Pegasus, of course, the immortal winged horse and child of Poseidon and Medusa from Greek mythology, represents freedom and power. It had been the name given by the Bristol Aeroplane Co. to its supercharged nine-cylinder one-row air-cooled radial engine from the 1930s and which, according to an advertisement at the Paris Aero Show, the Pegasus S-3 engine fitted in a Vickers "Vespa" Biplane flown by a Flt.-Lieut. C.F. Uwins on 16 September 1932 set a Fédération Aéronautique Internationale world altitude record of 43,976 feet, some 8.33 miles high. A fitting new logo to now adorn the *408*.

In less than three weeks and having covered a further 1,477 hard miles it was back in the workshop to have new bolts fitted to the right-hand steering arm, two new wiper blades, the engine oil changed to BP long life, a filter change and a new left-hand side front headlamp unit fitted. On 6 December, with 4,781 miles on the odometer, the 4,000 mile service was carried out. The rear axle alignment was checked along with the front wheel caster, camber and toe-in reset.

Just over one month later after more hard driving 408/1 was back on 9 January 1964 for its 6,000 mile service. The front steering arms were checked, and new front brake callipers fitted along with a Marchal horn. Things were a bit quieter in January and on the last day of the month, having travelled just 161 miles since 9 January, a repair was made to the passenger side rear window, the handbrake was checked and reset and the brakes were bled.

The 408 did not visit the workshop in February and its next visit was not until nearly two months later on 24 March 1964 and by now the speedo reading was at 8,414 miles. Car number one was certainly being put through its paces and no doubt the gremlins that were being sorted and rectifications being made were implemented in the cars following it each week out of the Filton factory. The 8,000 mile service was carried out as was a fair amount of remedial work to the squeaking water pump, the hose clips, the tick over and engine hunting, the brake callipers, brake pads and handbrake, the carburettor, the steering box, the whining differential. The clock was serviced, the rust on the door hinges cleaned off, the driver's seat cushion raised to give a better driving position, the rattling headlamp rim on the driver's side was resecured, and the leak causing both driver and passenger's feet becoming wet in a downpour was sorted out. Finally, the car was given a good wax and polish. Back in the workshop a month later in April the tick over was speeded up, the indicator lever repaired, and another leak and rattle sorted. This time the back of the driver's seat was repadded. At 9,100 miles four new Avon tyres set at a pressure of 29 lbs were fitted along with the wheels from 407 PHT. 407 PHT is shown pictured on page 194 of the eccentric L. J. K. Setright's *A Private Car, An Account of the Bristol* published in 1999 by Palawan Press and awarded the Montagu of Beaulieu Trophy by the Guild of Motoring Writers that year. However, as *The Spectator* review of the two-volume definitive history of the Bristol marque said, 'Were photographs to fade from being looked at, I would have some explaining to do ... it is the text, however, that most intrigues and entrances. Setright is as idiosyncratic, as original as obstinately traditional as radically conservative and as a technically astute as his subject.'

Bristol was obviously trying out different configurations and set ups with this car as the 408 would have been fitted with Dunlop tyres before being switched to the Avon Turbospeed as worn many of the fastest cars of the time, and on its next visit to the workshop some of the padding in the back of driver's seat fitted a few weeks earlier was now taken out again. For its 10,000 mile service (at odometer reading 11,051 miles) more experimental adjustment work was carried out along the lines of 407 PHT, with the exhaust tail pipe ends cut to match the previous model's, while at 11,818 Dunlop tyres on the original wheels were refitted and then again at 12,399 miles the car was reshod once again with Avon tyres and tubes. All this work was being carried out at the end of 1964 just about the same time as another 408 was being despatched from the Filton Factory. I purchased this car in June 2015 from Western Australia before realising that the total restoration was beyond my capabilities and purse and reselling it at auction in October the same year. The Advice of Despatch notice shows that car number 408-1-043, engine number 949-23228C, chassis number 408-7043, the forty-third of the eighty-six cars produced, was despatched on 24 November 1964 to Messrs Anthony Crook Motors Ltd, The Roundabout,

The sorry state of Bristol 408-7043 showing its bones. (Jeremy Best)

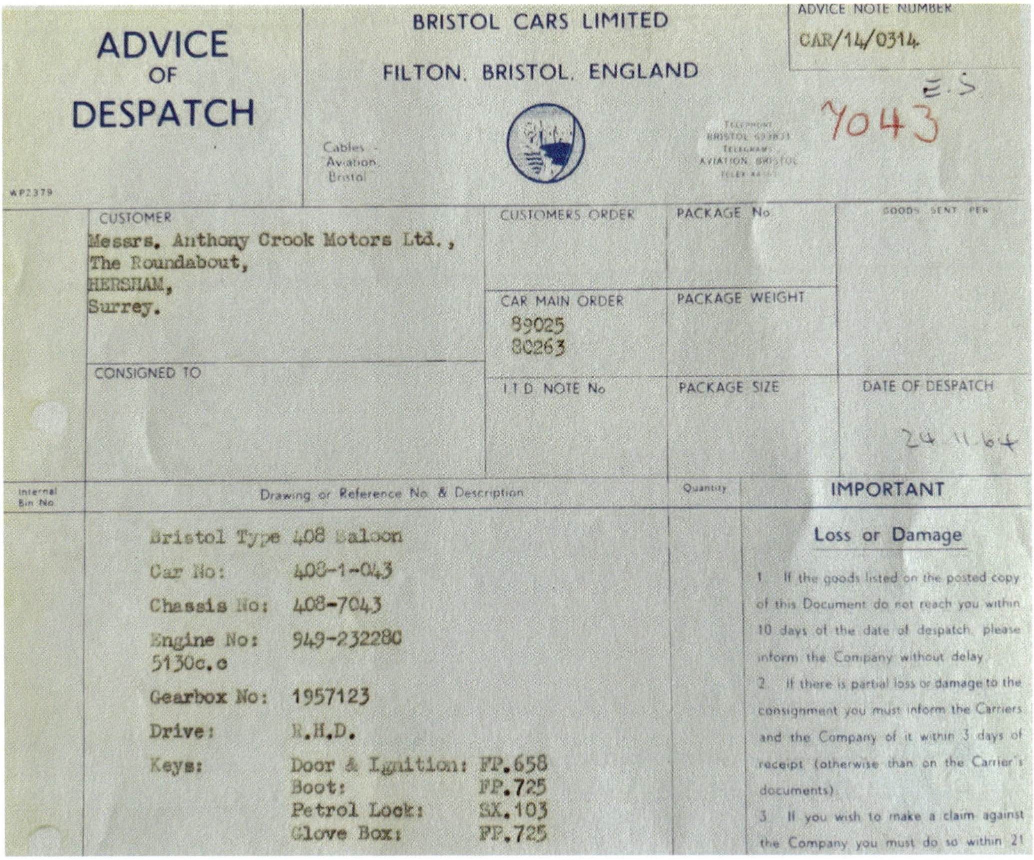

ADVICE OF DESPATCH

BRISTOL CARS LIMITED
FILTON, BRISTOL, ENGLAND

Cables - Aviation Bristol

WP2379

ADVICE NOTE NUMBER CAR/14/0314

E.S
7043

CUSTOMER
Messrs. Anthony Crook Motors Ltd.,
The Roundabout,
HERSHAM,
Surrey.

CUSTOMERS ORDER

PACKAGE No

GOODS SENT PER

CAR MAIN ORDER
89025
80263

PACKAGE WEIGHT

CONSIGNED TO

I.T.D. NOTE No

PACKAGE SIZE

DATE OF DESPATCH 24.11.64

Internal Bin No	Drawing or Reference No. & Description	Quantity
	Bristol Type 408 Saloon	
	Car No: 408-1-043	
	Chassis No: 408-7043	
	Engine No: 949-232280	
	5130c.c	
	Gearbox No: 1957123	
	Drive: R.H.D.	
	Keys: Door & Ignition: FP.658	
	Boot: FP.725	
	Petrol Lock: SX.103	
	Glove Box: FP.725	

IMPORTANT

Loss or Damage

1. If the goods listed on the posted copy of this Document do not reach you within 10 days of the date of despatch, please inform the Company without delay.

2. If there is partial loss or damage to the consignment you must inform the Carriers and the Company of it within 3 days of receipt (otherwise than on the Carrier's documents).

3. If you wish to make a claim against the Company you must do so within 21

Advice of Despatch for 408-7043. (James Nicholls)

Hersham, Surrey. Finished in single tone heather grey (code M.606) with red upholstery (code DR.3171), it came with the additional features of heater unit, windscreen washer and cigar lighter, and was also supplied and fitted with electric window winders. This car was first registered on 9 December 1964 at the same time that number one had nine pints of antifreeze added with 16,776 miles on the clock.

January 1965 at 18,100 miles during the 20,000 mile service routine work was done including fixing a small rattle in the dashboard and changing the radiator, which was leaking. More interestingly though further research and development was being carried out in anticipation of the launch of the Bristol 409, which would take place later in 1965. Girling servo assisted brakes were implemented as opposed to the original Dunlop 11¼-inch discs, along with the rear axle changed. At 20,588 miles the rear axle was reported as being noisy and this was changed once more when the speedo read 21,334. The new axle B65-153 was reported as 'noise level satisfactory, practically inaudible, Axle B65 – 153 v slight 25 – 28 and 58 – 61 m.p.h.'

Research was also being undertaken on the Selectaride adjustable suspension and at 21,811 miles according to the details of work carried out on the Record Card the instruction was to 'Fit special Selectarides (from Devel)'. These were removed on 1 June 1965 at 23,006 miles and returned to Devel and original Armstrong Selectaride refitted. Later that month 409 type front suspension arms from development were fitted to 408/1. On 29 September with a further 3,600 plus miles added to the speedo French Cibié high performance headlamp units with inner quartz iodine bulbs were fitted for testing. With the launch of the 409 in late 1965 we see the end of 408/1's time as a mule, with various improvements and refinements tested on 408/1 brought to fruition on the 408 MkII (which accounted for just the last fifteen units of 408 production with the slightly larger 318 cu.in, 5,211 cc engine as opposed to the 313 cu.in of 5,120 cc), and the 409, such as the adoption of the Girling rather than Dunlop braking system. By March 1966, with 31,921 miles on the clock and fitted with new Avon tyres and tubes, the headlamps reconverted to standard, the fire extinguisher removed and the Marchal horn removed, and the car thoroughly detailed, 408/1 had been returned to standard and made ready for sale.

5

Fit for a Gentleman

As we have already seen the Bristol cars were slightly idiosyncratic and appealed to motorists who wanted something different, out of the ordinary, and redolent of the exclusive gentleman's club such as Brooks's, founded in 1762, White's from 1693, the more egalitarian Royal Automobile Club on Pall Mall from 1897, all within a stone's throw of each other, or perhaps P. G. Wodehouse's fictitious Drones Club, haunt of Bertie Wooster, Bingo Little, Pongo Twistleton, Monty Bodkin, Oofy Prosser and their chums. Leather and walnut are *de rigueur* and inside the cabin of a Bristol is as much a place to hide from the harsh realities of the outside world as the Drones Club was for Bertie to avoid Aunt Agatha, the Lady Worplesdon, for as Wodehouse's protagonist would say, 'Aunts aren't gentlemen'.

The Armstrong Selectaride suspension on a Bristol 408 while not unique – it was also used on contemporary Jensen models and the Aston Martin DB4, 5, and 6 – was very special in that it was possible to change the suspension setting to suit the conditions of the road and required ride comfort. Perhaps the best way to explain the operation of the system is to quote directly from page 44 of The Bristol Type 408 Car Instruction Manual:

> ARMSTRONG SELECTARIDE electrically controlled absorbers are fitted to the rear suspension and are operated by the switch on the dashboard. See Page 6 & 7. The switch must be turned clock-wise only, as indicated by the arrows on the bezel between the stations. The 'SOFT' station is recommended for leisurely cruising while high speeds could demand the firm suspension provided for by Station 4. Intermediate degrees of damping are provided for by Stations 2 and 3. If, by any chance it is desired to go from a 'SOFT' ride to a firm ride (4) then the switch must be turned through the intermediate stations, as indicated by the arrows, in order to reach it. The switch must not be turned back (anti-clockwise).
>
> Note: If the Selectaride switch is moved with the ignition off, turn the switch through one full revolution with the ignition on before selecting the desired setting. When operating the switch do not hold the pointer in a position between the marked stations into which it indexes.

The interior of the Royal Automobile Club, Pall Mall, London, with a W. O. Bentley on display. (James Nicholls)

Plenty to go wrong then and with early 1960s electrics, the Selectaride would suffer from voltage drops on any bad earths in the car. Unfortunately, this often meant that one side would perhaps stay on a soft setting and the other side on a harder setting. Apparently once out of synch this was how they would remain, causing an uneven ride. This is what had happened at an odometer reading of 21,211 miles on 408/1 when the Car Service Record Card tells us that they were 'sticking' and again at 21,334 miles when the Card note read '?Rear selectarides.'. To this end today it means that to find electrically adjustable Selectaride on a Bristol 408 or Aston Martin DB5 is very rare indeed, with most having been replaced with more conventional shock absorbers and the magic button on the dashboard now defunct.

The 408 was fitted with very strong and sturdy Torque-Flite automatic transmission. Trademarked by the Chrysler Corporation, the most likely apocryphal story goes that the only reason Bristol selected it was because when the first Chrysler engine was sent from Canada it still had, due to an oversight or laziness, the gear box attached. This seems highly unlikely as the engine and gearbox work well together creating a perfect union so why would Bristol not have taken the package holus-bolus in any event? Whatever the rationale, the power unit and transmission were an ideal marriage for the 408, but Bristol being Bristol it did need to come with the Bristol touch of difference to set the car apart from the hoi polloi, for it came with push button gear selectors. By means of a series of buttons located on the dashboard to the right of the steering wheel it was possible to select and hold the required gear in this order from left to right: Reverse indicated by the letter 'R', Neutral (N), Drive (D), Second (2), or First Gear (1). To quote from the Instruction Manual once again, 'With the torque-flite transmission, the clutch pedal has been eliminated from the

An image of the Push Button Gear Selectors on the dashboard of the Type 408. Notice the absence of P for park. (James Nicholls)

car controls, and push button gear selectors located on the instrument panel provide the driving control. The driver simply pushes the desired button and applies the engine power by means of the accelerator pedal for complete control of car direction and application of the driving power.'

One omission on the 408 that was rectified on the 409 and subsequent models was the addition of a Park (P) setting, which enabled the vehicle to be held on steep slopes and hills without relying solely on the handbrake to stop one from rolling forwards or back. This is quite an important safety feature and something to be aware of when driving a Bristol 408 today. Apparently this was quite common on contemporary cars fitted with the similar Chrysler push button arrangement.

The Bristol marque has always been slightly individualistic and one aspect that highlights this is the choice of steering wheel used. From the earliest Bristol 400 exhibited at the January 1947 Geneva Motor Show the Bluemels was the company's steering wheel of choice. Originally an East End of London manufacturer of umbrellas, in 1911 Bluemels moved to Wolston, five and a half miles outside Coventry, the home of much of England's burgeoning car manufacturing industry. As such it was ideally placed to utilise its celluloid moulding skills in producing steering wheels for the likes of Lagonda, Alvis, MG and, of course, Bristol, even going as far as creating the steering wheel for Sir Malcolm Campbell's land speed record breaking *Bluebird.* From the 401 model onwards a distinctive two-spoke steering wheel was used, which further enhanced the aeronautical influence of the Bristol

The Bluemels steering wheel typically seen on the Bristol. Here shown on a left-hand drive Type 406. (Bonhams)

Close-up of Sir Malcolm Campbell seated in the cockpit of Bluebird holding a Bluemels steering wheel, 29 May 1947. (The Associated Press Ltd)

models and allowed the driver a clearer view of the car's instrument binnacle. This same style wheel was also used in the rare and seductive 402 and right through the 1960s with the eight-cylinder cars. Another steering wheel that might be found on a Bristol, though not factory fitted, is of course a Nardi such as fitted on the 406 Zagato, providing even more inimitable Italian style. Enrico Nardi was the very first Ferarri test driver, and in 1947, along with Renato Danese, founded ND, Nardi Danese, in Turin. In 1958 Nardi started working with Enzo Ferrari and thus many Ferrari cars are fitted with Nardi steering wheels.

Other idiosyncrasies of the Bristol are the positioning of the battery and spare wheel. For the rare 404 model onwards and with the development of Bristol's only two-seater of which just fifty short chassis units of this high performance coupé were built, Bristol came up with a clever space saving method of housing these essential but sizeable components. As 25 September 1953 issue of *Autocar* stated in its article entitled 'An Exciting New Bristol',

> The main body framing is a composite structure of steel, wood and light alloy, each material being used where its particular characteristics are most suitable. Light

A Ferrari featuring a Nardi steering wheel. (James Nicholls)

> frames welded to the to the main chassis frame support the scuttle structure, which consists of a bulkhead suitably braced and boxed by means of two side plates which form the inner panels for the spare wheel and battery compartments. A subframe running in front of the main front cross member, and suitably braced by diagonal tubes, connects with horizontal members running from the scuttle to the front of the car, which in turn are connected to the light alloy wing vallances. Both front side panels and the complete front body panel are welded and worked to form a complete unit before they are attached to the framework. The size of the resulting panel is reduced and construction is simplified by an ingenious arrangement of hinged body side panels which form cover plates for compartments behind the front wheel arches that house the spare wheel and electrical components.

John Bolster talking of the same model that exists '…among well-to-do connoisseurs for a more compact car than the "403"' in the 16 October 1953 of *Autosport* magazine also makes mention of, 'The spare wheel on the Bristol 404 is housed in a readily accessible compartment in the near-side front wing.' To this sentence taken directly from the Bristol Aeroplane Company listing on Stand 160 of the October 1953 Earls Court Motor Show, Bolster might well have also added, 'battery housed in similar compartment in off side front wing'. This is the same configuration to be found on the Bristol 408 and beyond.

With such distinctive and innovative engineering, aircraft grade build quality, and attention to luxury detailing why is Bristol then an almost forgotten marque? After all, as

Above: Bristol 408-7001 in Perth, Western Australia, showing the unique battery and spare wheel compartments. (James Nicholls)

Right: The ever-debonair polyglot Simon Kidston acting as the master of ceremonies at the Concorso d'Eleganza Villa d'Este. (James Nicholls)

Simon Kidston, known around the world as a multilingual classic car commentator and columnist, consultant and entrepreneur who has built up a globally renowned business specialising in the sale of the most valuable cars in existence, says, 'Throughout motoring history there have been only a handful of connoisseur's cars, such as Bentley's R-Type Continental or Citroën's SM. Bristol, though, is quite possibly the only connoisseurs' marque…'.

Unfortunately, or fortunately, depending upon one's point of view, being an expert judge in matters of taste does not necessarily reflect in the market price of vehicles. So, despite the pedigree, made up of the condition, provenance, rarity, desirability, history and originality, of the Bristol 408 why is it worth perhaps just one tenth of the price of a contemporary Aston Martin DB5 today when in 1963 it cost more? The vagaries of the classic car market are manyfold but without delving too deeply into socio-economic rational there are other forces at play that make cars such as the Mercedes-Benz 300 SL, Lamborghini Miura, or Aston Martin DB5 more sought after. Firstly, all three of the manufacturers cited still make cars today. They, like Jaguar, Ferrari, Maserati, Bentley, and Rolls-Royce, have a continuous linear history whereas Bristol, like other great marques such as Alvis, Lagonda and Lancia, have fallen by the wayside. The person who has a modern Aston Martin and everything

The avant-garde Citroën SM in front Hyde Park Barracks, Sydney. (Sydney Harbour Concours d'Elegance)

else they may need likes to feel the weight of history behind them and so is attracted to the thought of the heritage and traditions of the brand which they have bought into.

There are, of course, cultural influences too. It may be that the DB5 is ultimately a better car than the 408. Indeed, at the time it was more popular with 898 saloons made to eighty-six by Bristol. Both though are elegant Grand Tourers, very fast and with four seats, big boots, and big fuel tanks capable of long journeys in comfort and style. Yet only one carried the endorsement and imprimatur of James Bond, and the transmedia franchise that is 007. To quote Simon Kidston again, 'In Silver Birch one of the world's most recognisable cars. Thanks to 007, put Aston Martin on the map and on most schoolboys' letter to Santa. For the Corgi model, at least'.

Heritage, tradition, and even race pedigree are important factors in why and how people buy motorcars today. How else can a modern reinvented Chinese brand such as MG use the slogan 'value since 1924' when there is no correlation between the famous octagon logo of Morris Garages, founded that year and which won its class in the 1933 Mille Miglia with the MG K3 driven by George Eyston and Count Jonny Lurani and at the RAC Tourist Trophy the following year when driven by the legendary Flying Mantovan Tazio Nuvolari, which was holder of so many speed records, and created the

A 'model' Aston Martin DB5 at Battersea Power Station. (Aston Martin)

The 1933 MG K3, which was driven by George Eyston and Count Jonny Lurani to a class victory in the 1933 Mille Miglia. Here the car is seen eighty years later at the Motel Nautilus on the shores of Lake Como after competing in the 2013 Mille Miglia. (James Nicholls)

MGB (the car 'your mother wouldn't like'), with the anodyne family SUVs now being built – other than the name itself?

The James Bond factor is certainly very important when it comes to the values of classic Aston Martins and can be seen to a lesser extent with such relationships as Simon Templar, the Saint, as portrayed by Roger Moore with the Volvo P1800, and Inspector Morse's Jaguar Mk 2. But what of Bristol? Is there any celebrity endorsement? Not really, I am afraid, apart from Jean Simmons and Stewart Granger in their pair of 402s, and *The Inspector Lynley Mysteries*, the tv drama from the turn of this century featuring Detective Inspector Tommy Lynley, 8th Earl of Asherton (played by Nathaniel Parker). This polished peer (who in the original books drives a Bentley) starts off in a Jensen Interceptor but soon upgrades to a Bristol 410 as befits his position in society as a Lord of the Realm. Celebrity status is few and far between and although the likes of Bono, Liam Gallagher, King Hussein of Jordan, Sir Richard Branson, and even Peter Sellers, whose girlfriend at the time, actress and model Patsy Kensit, chose the colour scheme, are among those who have purchased and owned Bristols. While being very exclusive they are just too lacking in ostentation to be a celebrity chariot. Clark Gable in a Jaguar XK120 roadster, Tom Selleck as Magnum PI or Steve McQueen in a Ferrari they ain't, being more akin to an Oxbridge don's academic study than Hollywood Boulevardier or flaneur.

An example of a Bristol 410. Note the rather horrible after-market wing mirrors. (Jeremy Best)

The interior of Clark Gable's XK120 roadster, which he said he wanted like a baby wants candy. (James Nicholls)

6

The Magazines

While accepting that the Bristol 408 is not the motoring equivalent of the mondaine-about-town, it was still a motor car that generated considerable interest and was much sought after among the specialist press and was very well received at the time of its launch in late 1963. Chassis number 408/1 was used as the press car by Bristol for road testing by journalists. It was originally registered as 408 UHU. According to my unmarked copy of *I-Spy Car Numbers* book by Big Chief I-SPY, costing one shilling in 1968, this is a very apt number plate indeed. Obviously the 408 refers to the model number of the car, while UHU is, of course, the interjection 'yoo-hoo' first used in the early 1920s to attract someone's

Above: The I-Spy Car Numbers book enabling one to understand the relevance of 408 UHU and its connection to Bristol. (James Nicholls)

Left: The original number plate 408 UHU and ephemera of 408-7001. (James Nicholls)

attention. Closer investigation also tells us that HU is the index mark allotted to the Bristol County Borough Council to register vehicles. 408 UHU when it was launched certainly attracted the attention of the motoring press.

This car first appeared in 25 September 1963 edition of *The Motor* magazine of which Laurence E. Pomeroy, author of the esteemed *The Grand Prix Car* and president of the Vintage Sports Car Club, was a technical contributor. Priced at 1*s* 3*d*, volume 124 number 3201 of *The Motor* carried stories on the humble Morris 1100, a road test on the Sunbeam Alpine (series III), reports on motor sports events including the battle between Jaguar and Ferrari at the Tour de France Automobile, an article on the Frankfurt Motor Show, and under new cars for 1964 the Chevrolet Chevelle Malibu Super Sport, and the Bristol 408, which referenced the very large boot and also said, 'A short test demonstrated the effectiveness of the adjustable shock absorbers over varying road surfaces and the suitability of the Chrysler units. Acceleration on automatic could not be bettered by holding the individual gears and gear changes were scarcely noticeable. Wind tunnel testing of the body shape was justified by the absence of wind roar; the handling was steady and precise at all speeds, although the steering was a little heavier than might have been expected. This test also served to confirm the probability of the manufacturer's figure of 0–100 on 26 seconds.'

38 THE MOTOR September 25 1963

The BRISTOL 408

1964 Cars

THE new Bristol is a logical development of the 407. A redesigned body gives an up-to-date shape still in the tradition of the Bristol 400-series. A new frontal treatment houses four headlights while at the rear a revised lamp cluster and a wrap-round bumper help to distinguish the 408. A slightly squared roof-line gives an overall height an inch less than the 407.

Interior planning is unchanged, with reclining front seats and very comfortable back seat accommodation for two; seat belt attachment points are provided, but choice of make is left to the owner. The dashboard, with lockable glove pocket, is of polished wood with a separate nacelle housing a comprehensive set of instruments.

Cold air is ducted from a large plenum chamber which is supplied from a grille at the rear of the bonnet; hot air is provided by a Smiths heater which also draws from the plenum chamber.

The rear shock absorber settings can be varied by the Armstrong Selectaride system, operated by a four-position switch on the facia. A live rear axle is controlled by torsion bars and Watts linkage with telescopic shock absorbers; independent front suspension uses coil springs and transverse wishbones. Dunlop 11¼ in. disc brakes are fitted all round and are operated through a Lockheed tandem vacuum servo unit. Dunlop RS5 (6·00-16) tyres are fitted as standard.

The relatively light engine, incorporating the latest American thin-section cast iron foundry techniques, is basically a 313 Chrysler 5·13-litre V-8. Different camshaft configurations and an inlet manifold to take the four-choke Carter carburetter, give the Bristol version 250 b.h.p. (gross) at 4,400 r.p.m. and 340 lb. ft. torque at 2,800 r.p.m. This is coupled to the Chrysler Torqueflite 3-speed automatic transmission, as designed for this power unit.

Engine cooling is assisted by two thermostatically controlled Kenlowe electric fans which are accessible, with the horns, through an easily removed front grille.

A short test demonstrated the effectiveness of the adjustable shock absorbers over varying road surfaces and the suitability of the Chrysler units. Acceleration on automatic could not be bettered by holding the individual gears and gear changes were scarcely noticeable. Wind tunnel testing of the body shape was justified by the absence of wind roar; the handling was steady and precise at all speeds, although the steering was a little heavier than might be expected. This test also served to confirm the probability of the manufacturer's figure of 0-100 in 26 seconds.

(Above) the treatment of the four headlights is different, and the roof line is squarer and one inch lower than the 407. There is plenty of room for baggage in the large boot (left), and the revised lamp clusters remind one of the Humber Sceptre. The wrap-around bumper is also new.

Above left: The front cover of *The Motor* magazine, 25 September 1963, which featured 408-7001. (James Nicholls)

Above right: 408-7001 featured on page 38 of *The Motor*, 25 September 1963. Note the large boot capable of holding plenty of luggage. (James Nicholls)

Above left: An advertisement for the Bristol Type 408 featuring car number 408-1-001, which appeared in *Autocar* magazine on 27 September 1963. (James Nicholls)

Above right: An advertisement in *Autocar* on 27 September 1963 for Dunlop disc brakes and tyres as fitted to the Bristol 408 featuring car number 408-1–001. (James Nicholls)

Bristol also took the opportunity to run various advertisements extolling the virtues of the 408, referencing with Kenlowe Accessories its 'Thermostatic' electric cooling fan 'on the magnificent Bristol 408'; with Dunlop emphasising safety and performance when talking of the disc brakes and RS5 tyres 'of this fine, fast 5.2-litre car'; another house ad introducing the 'high performance with thoroughbred distinction luxurious full four-seater'; along with a list of distributors for the marque which included Bolton of Leeds, R. F. Fuggle established in 1906 in Bushey Heath, Hertfordshire, and of course Anthony Crook Motors Ltd giving 'performance comparisons' of the 407 against competitors Rolls-Royce, Daimler Majestic Major, Vanden Plas 4-litre, and the Mercedes-Benz 300SE and cordially inviting readers to view the new 408, which was, 'lower, shorter, superior, with even better streamlining, suspension and styling.'

Next to appear two days later on the newsstand on 27 September and competitively priced the same as *The Motor* was volume 119 number 3528 of *Autocar,* founded in 1895. *Autocar* carried the new for 1964 Vauxhall Viva (how well I remember being allowed to drive my father's new pale baby blue number) with inside cutaway drawings information and a massive amount of advertising for the same. In between a story entitled 'From Snow

Above left: The cover of *Autocar* magazine, 27 September 1963, which carried an article of the Bristol 408. (James Nicholls)

Above right: Car number 408-1-001 pictured in the article on the Bristol 408 in *Autocar*, 27 September 1963. (James Nicholls)

The author at the wheel of his father's Vauxhall Viva watched by his dog Boy, *c*. 1973. (Jack Lawrence Nicholls)

to Sunshine', a winter caravan trip to Morocco and the New Products Review highlighting DIY electric windows was the review of 408 UHU, which talked of 'The deception of shortening the car and yet making it look longer has been remarkably successful.' In among all the Vauxhall Viva pages could also be found the same advertisements for Bristol as in *The Motor*, plus another half page ad from The Hughes-Johnson Stampings company of Langley Green in Birmingham, which was pleased to 'gratefully acknowledge the opportunity afforded us of producing forgings for this new Mark'. Anthony Crook's advertisement had different copy in *Autocar* from that in *The Motor*. In this advert Crook asked the question, 'Who will buy the new 408?' The rather verbose answer in very small print was as follows:

> ...looking through the 'type' of clients buying the last model, we find no particular 'type'. It is not necessarily a matter of age (our youngest new 407 owner was 22, our oldest 74). Some said they bought it because it felt so safe, others because it was quieter (as well as cheaper to purchase and run) than other V.8-engined luxury cars, others said they had owned every previous model and each was better than the last. A few said it was because the car was not mass produced and thus remained fairly exclusive. One lady said it was entirely due to the wonderful interior comfort. Another owner said that since so much of his motoring was in town, he might as well sit in something really comfortable with a good automatic box! (Later adding that it was the best gear box he had ever handled.) Another said that he would never go back to a chassis-less car again and the BRISTOL was one of the very few cars with a chassis ... Another said it was wonderful value because his previous one lasted so long, and it was a hand-built car selling for much less than 'special bodied cars' ... and so the reasons went on...BUT there is something which appeals to everyone in a BRISTOL and this is surely the reason that the BRISTOL is rapidly becoming known as 'THE BEST ALL ROUND BRITISH CAR'.

The following year in December 1964 the glossy pages of *Cars Illustrated* (my copy stamped in capital letters on the cover 'Hackney Public Libraries Reference Department Not to be Taken Away'), priced at two shillings and sixpence, carried out a full report along with the Mercedes-Benz 300SE as one of the two *Cars On Test*. It was effusive in its praise: 'Although born of a fairly long line of cars whose appeal is in the connoisseur class, the Bristol 408 is comparatively little known. Perhaps because of this, it somehow seems to invite comparison with others that are known to set standards. Let us fall in with this idea by saying that in quality of manufacture it bears comparison with the best products of other British manufacturers of luxury cars, while in performance it is surely sufficient to remark that it will hold a 250GT 2+2 Ferrari over a standing half mile.'

Later in the article the writer goes on to say, 'Just how fast the Bristol is can be difficult to appreciate, so utterly fuss-free is it at all speeds. Even when accelerating hard, the silence of the engine and the slickness of the transmission mask much of the drama, but the push in the back can certainly be felt. It is not just a jerk, it is a long sustained push that tells of acceleration being maintained and hints at the meaning of a 470 lb/ton Tapley pull in top gear – higher, just to put the car in perspective, than that of an E-type Jaguar.'

The cover of *Cars Illustrated* magazine, December 1964, which featured the Bristol 408. Note the Hackney Public Libraries Reference Department stamp – not to be taken away! (James Nicholls)

The Bristol 408 and a Ferrari 250 GTE. An interesting comparison which in period showed that the 408 was no slouch over a ¼ mile. (James Nicholls)

The writer concludes the test saying, 'The car is very well-balanced, with just enough understeer for directional stability at high speed, and there is enough power on tap for some fairly advanced cornering techniques to be used. Steady drifts through long fast curves or rapid attitude reversals in roundabouts can all be included in the repertoire; but in practice the limits of cornering are imposed by consciousness of that £4,459 price tag!'

Finally on the matter of the written word in period I should mention that 408 UHU appeared on page 69 of the *1964 World Car Catalogue*, edited by Sergio D'Angelo and published annually by A.C.I., the Automobile Club of Italy. Listed under the variations and optional accessories was offered a 408 GT Zagato version offering 2+2 seats, 2.80 axle ratio, power-weight ratio 11.9 lb/hp 5.4 kg/hp, with a dry weight of 2,968 lb/ 1,346 kg, a saving of 616 lb or some 280 kg over the standard 408. The catalogue also listed practical instructions including use of 100 octane fuel, service intervals including a recommended oil change every 3,000 miles, tappet clearances, and tyre pressures of 29 psi front and rear for a medium load.

Of the 657 cars that one could buy listed in the 1964 catalogue with indices according to country and manufacture, to engine capacity, to maximum speed, and according

GREAT BRITAIN

408

Bristol

b

ENGINE CAPACITY 313.76 cu in, 5,130 cu cm
FUEL CONSUMPTION 18 m/imp gal, 15 m/US gal, 15.7 l × 100 km
SEATS 4 MAX SPEED 122 mph, 196.4 km/h
PRICE list £ 3,690, total £ 4,459

ENGINE front, 4 stroke; cylinders: 8, Vee-slanted at 90°; bore and stroke: 3.88 × 3.31 in, 98.5 × 84.1 mm; engine capacity: 313.76 cu in, 5,130 cu cm; compression ratio: 9; max power (SAE): 250 hp at 4,400 rpm; max torque (SAE): 340 lb/ft, 46.9 kg/m at 2,800 rpm; max number of engine rpm: 5,100; specific power: 48.7 hp/l; cylinder block: cast iron; cylinder head: cast iron; crankshaft bearings: 5; valves: 2 per cylinder, overhead, push-rods and rockers; camshaft: 1, at centre of Vee; lubrication: rotary pump, filter on by-pass; lubricating system capacity: 11 imp pt, 13.11 US pt, 6.2 l; carburation: 1 Carter AFB 3131S downdraught 4-barrel carburettor; fuel feed: mechanical pump; cooling system: water, 2 automatic thermostatically controlled fans; cooling system capacity: 36 imp pt, 43.13 US pt, 20.4 l.

TRANSMISSION driving wheels: rear; gearbox: Torqueflite automatic, hydraulic torque convertor and planetary gears with 3 ratios + reverse, max ratio of convertor at stall 2.20, possible manual selection; gearbox ratios: I 2.45, II 1.45, III 1, rev 2.20; push button control on facia; final drive: hypoid bevel; axle ratio: 3.31.

CHASSIS box-type ladder frame; front suspension: independent, wishbones, coil springs, anti-roll bar, telescopic dampers; rear suspension: rigid axle, longitudinal torsion bars, trailing lower radius arms, upper torque arm, transverse Watt linkage, electrically adjustable telescopic dampers.

STEERING worm and roller; turns of steering wheel lock to lock: 4.

BRAKES disc (diameter 11.25 in, 286 mm), vacuum servo.

ELECTRICAL EQUIPMENT voltage: 12 V; battery: 72 Ah; alternator; ignition distributor: Autolite; headlights: 2.

DIMENSIONS AND WEIGHT wheel base: 114 in, 2,896 mm; front track: 53 in, 1,346 mm; rear track: 54.50 in, 1,384 mm; overall length: 193.50 in, 4,915 mm; overall width: 68 in, 1,727 mm; overall height: 59 in, 1,499 mm; ground clearance: 6.50 in, 165 mm; dry weight: 3,584 lb, 1,626 kg; distribution of weight: 53% front axle, 47% rear axle; turning circle (between walls): 39.6 ft, 12.1 m; tyres: 6.00 × 16; fuel tank capacity: 18 imp gal, 21.6 US gal, 82 l.

BODY saloon; doors: 2; seats: 4; front seats: separate, reclining backrests.

PERFORMANCE max speeds: 40 mph, 64.4 km/h in 1st gear; 70 mph, 112.7 km/h in 2nd gear; 122 mph, 196.4 km/h in 3rd gear; power-weight ratio: 14.3 lb/hp, 6.5 kg/hp; carrying capacity: 706 lb, 320 kg; acceleration: standing ¼ mile 16.2 sec, 0—50 mph (0—80 km/h) 6.6 sec; speed in direct drive at 1,000 rpm: 23.8 mph, 38.3 km/h.

PRACTICAL INSTRUCTIONS fuel: 100 oct petrol; engine sump oil: 10 imp pt, 12.05 US pt, 5.7 l, SAE 20 (winter) 30 (summer), change every 3,000 miles, 4,800 km; gearbox oil: 16 imp pt, 19.24 US pt, 9.1 l, automatic transmission fluid, change every 10,000 miles, 16,100 km; final drive oil: 3 imp pt, 3.59 US pt, 1.7 l, EP 90, change every 10,000 miles, 16,100 km; steering box oil: EP 90; greasing: every 6,000 miles, 9,700 km, 2 points; tappet clearances: inlet 0.010 in, 0.25 mm hot, exhaust 0.018 in, 0.46 mm hot; valve timing: inlet opens 13° before tdc and closes 55° after bdc, exhaust opens 51° before bdc and closes 17° after tdc; tyre pressure (medium load): front 29 psi, 2 atm, rear 29 psi, 2 atm.

VARIATIONS AND OPTIONAL ACCESSORIES 408 GT Zagato, 2 + 2 seats, 2.80 axle ratio, dry weight 2,968 lb, 1,346 kg, power-weight ratio 11.9 lb/hp, 5.4 kg/hp.

69

Car number 408-1-001 pictured in the World Car Catalogue (1964), published annually by the Automobile Club of Italy. (James Nicholls)

to price, just twenty-nine, of which one was the Aston Martin DB5 convertible, three were Mercedes-Benz, four were Maserati, two Ferrari, eight Bentley, and nine models of Rolls-Royce, cost more than the 408. The Ferrari 400 Superamerica was also more expensive, priced at 9,500,000 lire or £5,453 sterling calculated on the rate of exchange at the time, but not usually imported into Great Britain. Again, of the 657 listed just fifty-eight had a higher top speed than the 408's 122 mph, and of these the only British cars that were

The beautiful aerodynamic shape of the Ferrari Superamerica photographed at the 2022 Concorso d'Eleganza Villa d'Este. One of the few cars more expensive than a Bristol 408 in period. (James Nicholls)

faster were the Jaguar 3.8-litre S Type at 123 mph and the fibreglass Daimler SP 250 at 124 mph, while discernibly speedier were the Lagonda Rapide at 128 mph, the Lotus Elite GT at 130, the Jensen CV8 at 136, the Aston Martin DB5 and E Type Jaguars at 150 mph. The fastest was the USA variant of the AC Cobra, with 325 hp competition engine and quadruple Weber twin barrel carburettors, which was capable of an astonishing maximum speed of 174 mph or 280.1 km/h.

As an aside the British correspondent for the *World Car Catalogue* was Denis Jenkinson, the quintessential *Motor Sport* magazine journo who, as well as being one of Britain's first ever motor sport World Champions as the passenger in the 1949 Sidecar World Championship, won by Eric Oliver on his 600 cc Norton-Watsonian, was most famously the navigator for Stirling Moss's victorious record breaking drive in the Mercedes-Benz 300SLR to win the Mille Miglia in 1955 at an average speed of 98 mph over the 992-mile course from Brescia to Rome and back.

7
The Find

But what became of 408 UHU after it was sold by Bristol in early 1966? Unfortunately little is known for the period between 1966 and 1984 except that there had been at least three owners of the car. On 27 June 1984 we know from Department of Transport registration documents that it was purchased by Praveen Moman of No. 27 Cadogan Square, London, SW1. Moman was born in 1954 and grew up in Uganda and as part of the Asian community there was central to the opening up of East Africa. His family became refugees under the regime of the invidious dictator Idi Amin and escaped to the United Kingdom, where he studied at London and Cambridge University. Moman was a political and policy adviser in the European Union, British Government and European Government. He held posts working for Lord Cockfield, Vice President of the European Commission; Lord Heseltine, the Deputy Prime Minister; Lord Renton, Minister for the Arts; and Lord Newton, the Leader of the House of Commons. Later in 1997, remembering his walks as a young boy with his father Kuldip Rai Moman near Gahinga, he established Volcanoes Safaris, returning to his homeland and establishing ecological wildlife preservation safaris there and in Rwanda. He now lives between London, Uganda and Rwanda, but no longer drives a Bristol 408, having sold it on 7 December 1987 through Chelsea Cars of Wandsworth, London, SW18, to Marcus Rawlinson of Little Shelford in Cambridge. As the original tax discs from the period show, Rawlinson had to drive to Great Shelford to register the 408, whereas Moman popped down to Sloane Square.

Rawlinson paid £6,400 for 408 UHU: the price included a twelve month warranty and a 6,000-mile interval service, and it was registered in his name on 14 December 1987 still carrying its original registration number and plates. By this time though the car had, sometime in the past, been painted in non-metallic mid blue (perhaps the factory pastel blue) from its original gunmetal grey and silver two-tone. On moving to Western Australia, Rawlinson took the decision to bring his Bristol with him. According to the Department of Transport Test Certificate carried out on 21 September 1992 the odometer reading was 38,388. The *Berlin Express* left Tilbury Docks on 2 January 1993 bound for Fremantle near Perth in Western Australia with 408 UHU in a 20-foot container on board. The insured value for the vehicle was £12,000, while customs charges were AU$2,614.73 paid prior to arrival. 408 UHU arrived in Australia on 30 January 1994 and was released

Road tax discs for Bristol 408 car number 408-1-001 showing Sloan Square, London, when owned by Praveen Moman, and Great Shelford, Cambridgeshire, when owned by Marcus Rawlinson in England. (James Nicholls)

by the Australian Quarantine and Inspection Service on the 4 February. Rawlinson, now of Woodlands in WA, registered it as 8PO-545.

In May 1995 work was carried out on the brakes and in 1997 on the front shock absorbers and steering mechanism and the engine and gearbox removed and refitted. In 1999 electrical work was carried out and it was at this period of ownership that the wheel rims were also repainted. Rawlinson maintained the vehicle well as is evidenced by the fact that in 2001 408 UHU took part in the tour celebrating the Centenary of Federation of Australia, driving from Perth to Canberra, a distance of over 3,700 km. Leaving on Saturday 14 April 2001 with the odometer at 50,850 miles, it was one of 1,200 pre-1976 vehicles from all over Australia that gathered for a festival between 26th and 29th of that month in the nation's capital. Not only was the first Bristol 408 ever built kept mechanically sound it was also looked after cosmetically, with the interior being retrimmed in May 2004 at a cost of AU$12,760 in the correct fashion but in red hide rather than the original warm stone colour, which was now split and beyond repair. This new red leather interior worked well with the pastel blue exterior and the car was one of those featured in the promotional materials for the 2013 Picnic in the Park Classic Car Show held on 28 April at Whiteman Park under the auspices of the Council of Motoring Clubs, and on Sunday 18 May 2014 at the 25th Annual British Car Day held at Gingin, 80 km north of Perth, where well over 700 cars were on display.

I purchased my first Bristol 408 sight unseen from a chap in Western Australia who had imported it from the UK and had then decided to start to restore it. He should have left well alone because all he had done was made a considerable mess of the car – it was in better condition before he had started than when he abandoned the project. Car number 408-1-043 (the forty-third built of eighty-six units), chassis number 408-7043 with engine number 949-23228C, was supplied in heather grey with red upholstery and came with the additional features of a heater unit, windscreen washers and cigar lighter, as well as an electric window. It was despatched from the Filton Factory on 24 November 1964 to Anthony Crook Motors, who supplied it to its first owners when it was registered on 9 December 1964.

Having sold 7043 unreserved at auction for AU$11,000 in October 2015 I was now on the look out for a more complete example of the marque. In April 2016 I flew to Perth to visit a client and decided to look at 7001, which was now being offered for sale by Marcus Rawlinson. Meeting by Cottesloe Beach in the car park of the Ocean Beach Hotel I felt quite happy in front of my old apartment where thirty years previously I had been a cricket professional on my first visit to Australia. The car looked in quite good shape and when I test drove it it went well around the streets of my old stomping ground. Marcus was a nice chap to deal with but I thought his asking price a little high and if truth be told I was a little disappointed that it was no longer in its original colour scheme. I was also unable to locate the engine number and was concerned that it no longer retained its original engine. I flew home to Sydney undecided.

The fact that I had not been able to check the engine number 949-23439C properly made up my mind upon reflection not to proceed at that time. Later that month Rawlinson showed the car to Commander Peter Hoskin, Royal Australian Navy retired, of Mawson in Canberra, who had a vehicle inspection report undertaken on 22 April 2016. There were only a few minor ailments and Commander Hoskin decided to proceed with the purchase

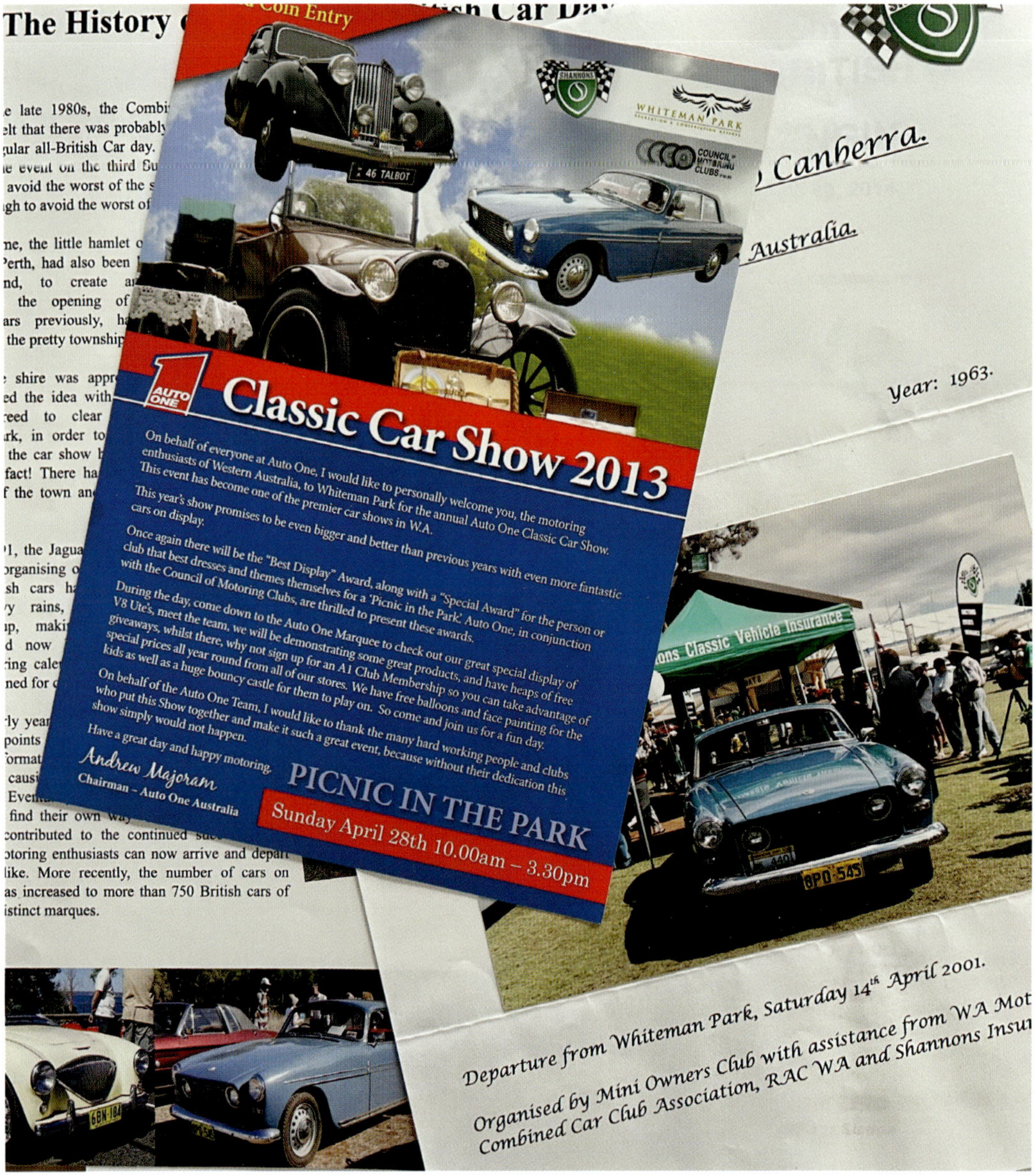

Ephemera relating to various shows at which car number 408-1-001 was a key exhibit during its time in Western Australia. (James Nicholls)

of 7001 in May. With minor remedial work being carried out to rectify the faults found out at inspection, an AU$4,000 deposit was paid on 9 June, with the remainder of the agreed AU$43,000 purchase price paid on 15 June. On Friday 17 June Commander and Mrs Hoskin flew to Perth to pick up the car from Hovea in the Shire of Mundaring, 30 km east of the state capital, where it now resided. The plan was to finalise everything, pick up the Bristol and visit the nearby York Motor Museum before making a nice holiday trip

The first Bristol 408, in the car park at the Ocean Beach Hotel, Cottesloe, Western Australia, when owned by Marcus Rawlinson. (James Nicholls)

home. Unfortunately, it was not plain sailing, and the Bristol was not ship-shape for the retired naval couple. The next day the Bristol developed a significant gearbox issue that had to be rectified, with the repaired car finally making it back to Canberra in the ACT in September, where it was registered as YMC75A before being re-registered in May 2017 as BR408.

Marcus Rawlinson had looked after 7001 very well indeed (and paid for the necessary repairs when he on sold it to the Hoskins), but Commander Hoskins took the maintenance to the next level. During his service in the Royal Navy and the Royal Australian Navy he had been a mechanical engineer charged with the maintenance of ship and submarine engines. He had also owned a succession of admirable classic cars including Bristols and a wonderful AC Aceca. He immediately and systematically set about going through every detail in the car as the extensive history file during his tenureship quantifies. For example, he had the rear-view mirror post of six parts chrome polished. Each and every item down to

A 1956 AC Aceca with its Bristol engine, of the type once owned by Commander Hoskins. (James Nicholls)

the last cent, or penny when parts were purchased from the UK, is itemised and recorded. The beautiful red leather was fed; the brake pedal rubber replaced; everything waxed or greased as necessary; a cracked lens replaced; workshop manuals purchased; oil leaks identified; gearbox, brakes and suspension overhauled; new carpets and boot mat fitted; carburettor overhauled; wood veneer panels sanded, stained and re-lacquered; the clock repaired (how rare it is to find a classic car with the Smiths clock still able to tell the time); the wheels repaired and repainted (if in the incorrect colour of metallic blue rather than the correct silver); a correct grommet here and a washer there; the engine mounts replaced; the boot locking mechanism repaired; EZ power steering fitted without compromising the originality of the vehicle or its integrity but making for ease of use; door handles; a new windscreen and rubbers fitted; the correct new old stock heating and ventilation system installed; and everything down to the last nut, bolt, screw, gasket and fuse checked, itemised and fixed or replaced as required.

The Commander, in true naval fashion, also kept a logbook itemising every trip taken in the car, which included a rally to Brisbane in Queensland, with his wife covering the 3,000-km round trip there and back home to Canberra, which went off without a hitch and in comfort. Every mile, litre of petrol, pint of engine oil (Penrite HPR3020W6) was dutifully recorded along with miles per gallon for each trip undertaken. Without a doubt

The original Radiomobile push button radio in the dashboard of Bristol 408-1-001. (James Nicholls)

the significant remedial work undertaken by this remarkable gentleman has helped to preserve the integrity and shelf life of this important motor car. My only criticism of his custodianship is the painting of the rims in the incorrect colour (though they look rather good, they need to be returned to the original) and the upgrading of the original Radiomobile push button radio and single speaker with a cassette player so that he and his wife could listen to audio books on longer journeys. Of course, doing things in the proper fashion he had the foresight to keep the original.

Meanwhile, four years later, having regretted my original decision not to purchase 7001, I was looking for a Bristol 408. I even contacted Marcus Rawlinson to see if he was still in possession of the car. The answer came back no; he had sold it to a person in Canberra. I did find a rather nice 1966 409 in England near to where my sister and brother-in-law live. Charles was duly dispatched to check it out and he gave it the thumbs up. I nearly purchased it in the middle of 2020 but decided to check in Australia one last time to see if there was anything available here. I duly contacted the Bristol Owner's Club of Australia (BOCA) to see if there might be a 408 preferably, 409 or 410 available. Lo and behold, the response came back that a gentleman in Canberra was looking to sell his 408. I was duly supplied with contact details. I received the following reply: 'I have a 408 Mk 1 which I have owned for 5 or so years and have been doing a lot of work recovering the car from

Bristol 408-1-001 in its pastel blue livery in Mawson, Canberra, when owned by Commander Hoskins. (James Nicholls)

a period of little use in WA. I could be tempted to sell if the price was right as I am over 80 years and finding it difficult to crawl under the car, or more precisely, to get up again!', along with a photograph of a familiar-looking blue 408.

On 8 August 2020 I flew from Sydney to Canberra to be picked up at the airport by Commander Hoskin in 7001. The car was very nice indeed and having this time been able to locate and verify the original engine number I agreed to purchase it and despite the global pandemic at that time was able to fly to Canberra again on Monday 17 August 2020 to pick up the car. On a beautiful sunny Australian winter's day, I undertook the three-hour journey home at a steady legal limit of 110 km/h without any issues, the Bristol maintaining its speed on the motorway as lesser vehicles fell behind on the uphill stretches. I knew I was on to a winner as soon as I left the Hoskin's home – at the first traffic lights I received a compliment and an admiring look from another motorist.

Once home in Sydney there were a few decisions to be made about 7001, which was now registered by me in New South Wales as CY84SK. Even though not in the original colour, the red hide interior of this Bristol was correctly done and in superb condition and even though I am a stickler for originality I was more than happy to live with it. The exterior pastel blue paint, however, was to my eye rather flat and dull looking and did not show off the car at its best. Having just purchased the car, however, I was not in a financial position to repaint it back to its original two-tone. I decided, mistakenly

Bristol 408-1-001 shortly after its arrival in Sydney. (James Nicholls)

as it turned out to be a false economy, to have the car 'wrapped' in vinyl to as close to the original colour as possible. While it might have created the desired effect and did not look that bad the process did not satisfy me and I knew it was only a short-term solution.

One of the first opportunities that I had to utilise the car on a really long run was in September 2020 on the inaugural Southern Classic Drive Rally, taking in the Blue Mountains, Nattai National Park, Jerrawangala National Park, the Great Eastern Escarpment, the Southern Highlands, Saddleback Mountain, and the Royal National Park over three days and 1,000 km of dramatic NSW scenery. There were even two track events at Luddenham Raceway and Wakefield Park Raceway for those with a need for speed. Suffice to say that 7001 performed flawlessly apart from a rear brake light bulb and was even able to test *Autocar* magazine's claims regarding a Ferrari 250 GTE that was also taking part. I can confirm that a 408 is not really at home on the track and does not have the same racing pedigree that had brought the marque such international success with the earlier six-cylinder cars. Truth be told the 408 is not truly a rally car either. While beautiful and very comfortable to drive on a tour with like-minded friends as on the Southern Classic, it was and is not a competition car in any way comparable with those Bristols of

Bristol 408-1-001 taking part in the inaugural Southern Classic Drive Rally in New South Wales. (James Nicholls)

A Bristol 408 is not really at home on the track – here 408-1-001 on the Southern Classic Drive is being put through its paces. (James Nicholls)

the late 1940s and early 1950s. In *The Autocar* (which first published in 1895 but changed its name to *Autocar* in 1962) 30 January 1948, the sports editor regretted that 'The best that can be done this year to remind readers of the most strenuous of all annual car rallies is this spirted drawing of an imaginary competitor in an imaginary 1948 Monte Carlo Rally climbing a mountain pass in Southern France. It would have been in this issue that "The Autocar" report of this annual pre-war event would have appeared. Great efforts to revive this famous competition for the first time since the war were made by Monsieur Anthony Nohges, the president of the International Sporting Club at Monaco. Regulations were issued in several languages, many prospective entries were received, but negotiations for the necessary petrol – although conducted at a diplomatic level – failed. However, the date is booked again for 1949 and the struggle to revive such international proving-tests will continue. Gordon Horner has depicted here the new 90 m.p.h. 2-litre Bristol, which would

Bristol-engined cars on the front row of the grid at the 2016 Goodwood Revival. (James Nicholls)

have made a promising competitor, and which might have added an early lustre to the already high reputation of this new British marque.'

In 1949 that lustre shone with an even brighter light, with Bristol 400s finishing third overall and being the first British car at the Monte Carlo Rally, second in the General Touring Class at the Targa Florio, third in the Touring Class at the Mille Miglia (with Count Lurani as one of the drivers along with H. J. Aldington in both these enormously important Italian events), first in class at both the Como Lario Hill Climb and at the Tuscany Cup, third in class at the Stella Alpina, and fourth and fifth in class and sixth overall at the Alpine Rally. A truly motoring annus mirabilis, never to be repeated, for the car division of the Bristol Aeroplane Company. And the man who had started it all off, Tony Crook, the man who would become Mr Bristol, drove a Bristol 400 in the 1948 Eastbourne Rally.

Subsequently, with its rear lights repaired, 7001 appeared in March 2021 at the Sydney Harbour Concours d'Elegance, which was a finalist in the Concours Event of Year category at the Historic Motoring Awards held in London in November 2021. This tasteful and sophisticated automobile looked very much at home on the curving driveway and luscious lawns of Swifts, the heritage-listed late Victorian castellated Gothic Revival mansion with its wonderful history, built in 1875 and described by the Australian Heritage Council as 'perhaps the grandest house remaining in Sydney'.

Bristol 408-1-001 on the luscious lawns of Swifts at the 2020 Sydney Harbour Concours d'Elegance. Note the Hispano-engined Delage in the background. (Sydney Harbour Concours d'Elegance)

Swifts, the Victorian castellated Gothic Revival mansion built in 1875, described by the Australian Heritage Council as perhaps the grandest house remaining Sydney. Note the very rare 1950 Bristol 402 behind the very rare 1954 Muntz Jet in the foreground at the Sydney Harbour Concours d'Elegance. (James Nicholls)

8

The Restoration

Bristol Cars being a private family company meant that it could do as it saw fit and conduct business in its own fashion, which was very different from other car builders being more akin to purchasing from a bespoke tailor. Under the tutelage of perfectionist Sir George White Bt II, grandson of the original founder of the Bristol Company Sir George, the aim was to produce cars as near to perfect as possible. Maintaining the manufacturing traditions of strict aviation industry standards, for every two workers on the assembly line at the Filton Works there was one inspector! During the 1920s and 1930s George White had been trying to encourage his father Sir Stanley to make cars but never quite succeeded. Sir George, who continued running the company until his tragic accident in 1969 when his stationery Bristol 410 saloon was hit by a lorry, always wanted to race cars according to his son, but Sir Stanley would not let him, so he took up racing boats instead with grudging paternal approval. In 1938 on 27 April he took the 4 litre world speed record, with the *Bristol Evening Post* newspaper headlines screaming 'SIR STANLEY WHITE'S SON SMASHES SPEEDBOAT RECORDS'. Although a far cry from the unlimited World Water Speed Record set by Malcolm Campbell later that year on Lake Hallwyl, Switzerland, when *Blue Bird K3* with its 2,000-hp Rolls-Royce engine achieved 130.94 mph (210.68 km/h), on Poole harbour George White guided *Bulldog III* with a hull designed by Vospers (which also built *Bluebird II [K4]* for Malcolm Campbell, *Bluebird K7* for his son Donald Campbell, and in the 1950s Royal Navy Brave Class fast patrol boats with Bristol Gas Turbine engines capable of 58 knots) and powered by a 3690 cc American Lycoming (another manufacturer of aeroplane engines) to a class record speed of 60.75 mph (97.76 km/h). According to the August 1938 issue of *Motor Boating,* on page 90 of the American magazine, 'Notification has been received from the International Motor Yachting Union that the official recognition as a world's record has been granted the performance of the Apel-designed Lycoming-powered 4-liter hydroplane Gray Goose, owned by George C. Cannon, of New Rochelle, N.Y., and driven in mile trials at Miami, on April 23, by Hugh Gingras, of Rockledge, Fla., at an average speed of 73.70 statute miles an hour. This is the second world's mile record granted to this class. Application for a world's record of 60.75 miles an hour, made on April 27, was granted to George White, of England, for his boat, *Bulldog III,* because his application

The Bluebird at speed during a trial run on 19 August 1937. (Fox Photos Ltd)

was received eight days prior to the American application which quickly superceded the British mark.'

In keeping with the idea of George White's endeavour to achieve perfection and with the 'wrap' not really doing 7001 justice I decided that the first 408 should be given a face lift. Happy with the mechanical aspects of the car and the interior but unhappy with exterior colour and paintwork and a few body blemishes, I contacted Justin Hills, the bespoke designer based in Taree on the mid north coast of New South Wales just over 300 km north of Sydney. Justin has an enviable reputation for just about being able to do anything you wish to a car body, as exemplified by these words from Ian Callum when he was director of design at Jaguar Cars: 'I have been watching the development of Justin's XK120 with great interest, The 120 of course is a car I know well. It is naturally very beautiful and with great heritage, so any modification had to be done with sympathy and with elegance. I think what Justin has done is not only beautiful but emphasises the very epitome of Jaguar.

Lower and sleeker and with just the right amount of drama and an amazing stance. The mechanical installation of the magical Jaguar V12 just adds to the magnificent beauty of this car. Sir William Lyons would have approved, I am sure.'

Justin is a true artisan who has had success at Salon Privé at Blenheim Palace; the Master of Customs in Detroit; at Quail Lodge during Pebble Beach Week; World's Most Beautiful Custom in Sacramento; at SEMA, the largest automotive trade show in the world in Las Vegas; at the Zoute GP in Belgium; at the Sydney Harbour Concours d'Elegance. He has displayed at the new Jaguar Design Studio at the company headquarters in Gaydon, Warwickshire and his work is on display at the National Museum of Australia in Canberra. This meant that I knew I was in safe hands to return 7001's aluminium body and paintwork to as near perfect original condition as it is possible to get in keeping with the philosophy of the three generations of the White family that created Bristol.

No easy task, however, and the process of how this is achieved is most interesting and perhaps best told in the words of Justin Hills himself.

Sir William Lyons would have approved I am sure. Justin Hills' amazing take on the Jaguar XK120. (Tom Shaw)

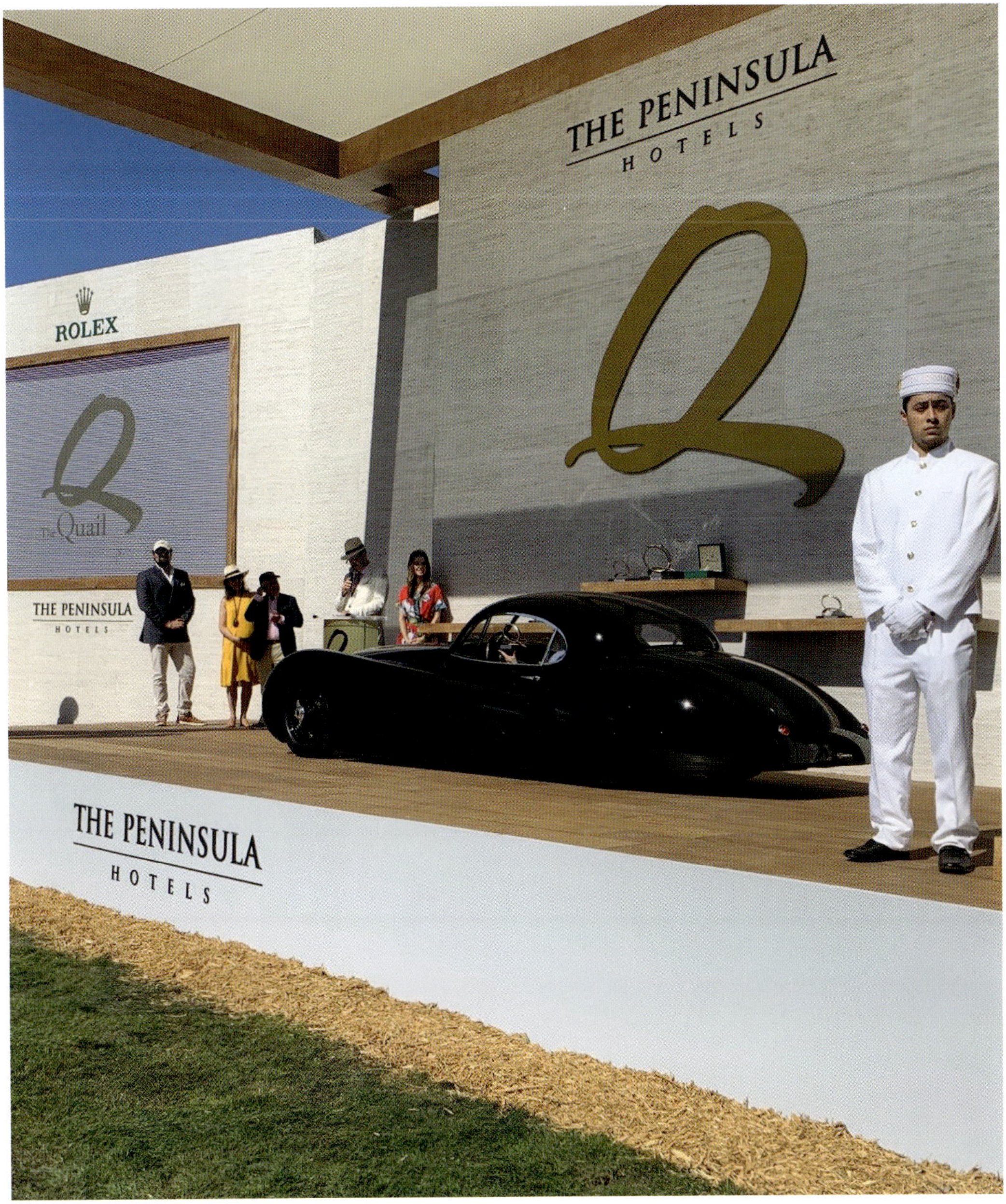

Justin Hills' Jaguar XK120 LM takes the honours at The Quail, A Motorsports Gathering, in 2019. (Angie Hills)

The first thing that was necessary to do with 7001 was to remove the vinyl wrapping that had been applied at the beginning of 2021. This was not as simple a job as it might first have appeared and indeed perhaps not even as easy as the quite difficult application procedure. The vinyl wrapping did not want to come off and when it did, it only came off in small pieces which made it a very time consuming job. The next

Justin Hills dwarfed by the trophy as the winner of The World's Most Beautiful Custom with his Dodge. (Justin Hills)

Artisan craftsman Justin Hills in front of a Bristol 410, which he is about to restore. (James Nicholls)

Prepping Bristol 408-1-001 for restoration at Hills & Co. in Taree, New South Wales. (Justin Hills)

undertaking after the removal of all the vinyl wrapping was to remove all the chrome handles and moulds including the distinctive Pegasus badges and side strips. The next stage after this was to mask up all the edges and begin the dirty job of manually removing all of the old paint on the car. Again, this was a very time consuming task as over the years there was a fair amount of old paint and some filler around the car. Having said that considering the car is nearly 60 years old it was in pretty good condition. Once all the old paint had been removed we went around each panel correcting any old repairs and welding up any cracks. Having recently completed a similar task on a Bristol 410 it would appear that these cars all seem to crack in approximately the same place in the plenum chamber situated just in front of the windscreen. Rolls-Royces from the same period suffer a similar fate.

7001 really was not in too bad a shape for a car of its age. The worst part of damage on the bodywork was situated in the boot lid. At one time perhaps the keys had been lost or someone tried to steal something out of the boot for where the boot catch is there were signs of a forced entry where it had been jimmied open at some point in its life causing quite nasty damage. This necessitated this area being cut out and all

Above: Masking up the 408 ready for restoration. Note the Bristol 410 in primer in the background. (Justin Hills)

Left: Justin Hills working on a repair for the 408 boot lid. (Justin Hills)

new pieces made and welded in. All our work is done by hand which is an important consideration knowing that the owner wanted the job to be completed properly but most importantly maintaining the intrinsic integrity of a vehicle such as this which was of course originally hand made.

So, with the alloy body now in much better shape and with a lot of foundation work carried out we applied an epoxy primer as a prophylactic barrier coat in order to keep any moisture out of the bodywork. This is an extremely important part of the whole undertaking as the alloy must be meticulously cleaned before anything else is applied. It is very easy for moisture or any other contaminative bodies to be trapped in at this early stage of the process which will ultimately cause corrosion problems or paint defects such as micro blistering later. Having allowed a period of a few weeks to allow the epoxy primer coat to settle and cure properly it was time for us then to go around the body with a polyester high fill spray filler. This is then sanded with course paper to create all the sharpness and the straight lines in the body. Any of the

During the restoration process, being made ready for paint at Hills & Co., Taree, NSW. (Justin Hills)

In the booth ready for the epoxy primer. (Monet Hills)

low spots found had filler reapplied and sanded once again and the exercise repeated again and again until the coachwork is flawless and the ready for its final primer. Again the sanding is all undertaken by hand, using a long sanding block of 1.2 metres to gain an even finish, with shorter sanding blocks used for the curved areas of the body. Once this operation was completed, we put 7001 back into the booth to be cleaned, wiped down and made ready for primer.

The next stage of the operation is the application of the 2k primer which is the foundation in providing a good key for the actual paintwork. This is really the last chance for blocking out those last small imperfections that might have shown up in the final rubbing of the polyester stage. Once the 2k primer has been sanded, not once but twice, first with a coarse paper and then finally with a very fine paper then our car is ready for paint. Fortunately, when we were disassembling and stripping 7001, removing the engine, bumpers, front and rear windscreens, rubbers, and chrome accoutrements etc, we found a very small remnant of the original paint inside one of the doors. This sample was just enough for us to be able to make a true match to the original colour. Very importantly the good thing about this small portion of paintwork that we found is that it had never before seen the light of day, so the final colour of 7001 will be true to the unfaded original gunmetal body colour first put on back in 1963.

Bristol 408-1-001, looking sharp and ready for primer. Note the almost perfect panel gaps achieved. (Justin Hills)

408-1-001 Ready for paint. (Monet Hills)

Once the primer has been allowed to settle over a period of a few weeks and has been sanded and checked it is time for cleaning and making sure that all the dust has been removed and blown away. The next task is that of masking. This needs to be done really cleanly again and very tightly in order that no little pockets or specks of dust or dirt are allowed to infiltrate the painting operation. Once masking has been completed and the booth itself has been cleaned and then sealed up and dust free, 7001 was wiped down with solvent wipes to ensure that there are no oily hand prints or any other contamination on the prime and surface. Now our car is ready to be painted, and in 7001's case in a base coat and then clear. First we applied three coats of base coat, of course allowing sufficient drying time between each coat. The first two coats to get good even coverage, with the final third coat added to get that beautiful even pattern throughout the metallic. Then we added five coats of clear coating. These are applied utilising a different technique adopted by a normal spray painter in a smash repair shop. The spray pattern used is slightly tighter and finer than that generally used in the motor industry which enables us to sand and buff to a very high level and to ensure the flat smooth finish required for top quality motor cars such as 7001 and my prize winners.

The sanding and buffing process is an incredibly important part of any top quality job and even though very time consuming is an area that must be undertaken very thoroughly. Firstly we start with 1,000 grit sandpaper and progressively work our way through to 3,000 grit. By following this method we ensure that buffing is made really easy with no fear of scratching of any sink back at a later stage. This is what has given 7001, and indeed all our customers vehicles, the beautiful lasting shine of the car as new in period.

I must admit that I have really enjoyed bringing 7001 back to peak condition. Not only has it been very satisfying to see this important motor car reinstated to a shape and order equivalent to that when it was new, I have also enjoyed it on a personal note. When I first saw 7001 I was not particularly over excited by the understated look of the car. Having carried out this restoration though, and immediately prior that of a Bristol 410, I have grown to appreciate the subtle and sophisticated lines and style of the 408 and why it picked up the coachwork award at the 1963 Earls Court Motor Show, along with the build quality carried out by those artisans back in Filton. For me though possibly the greatest joy has been working on the car myself along with my apprentice, rather than let my team do the work. It has been great to get my hands dirty on such a special car for James, especially working with that apprentice who happens to be my seventeen year old daughter Monet. I am sure she has learnt a lot working with me and I am really pleased with the way she is developing in the business, and she has also done all the boring and difficult to get at bits to save me having to do them! We have spent a great deal of quality father and daughter bonding time together – after all, to bring 7001 back to the resplendent condition and wonderful nick it is now in, sporting its correct two-tone paint work, has taken something approaching 700 man (and daughter) hours.

Once the paint on 7001 had been allowed to cure then came the task of putting it all back together again. Back in went the big red lump of its original engine #949-23439C, along with new rubbers all round, the re-installation of the original radio, and then as a final touch adding those unique number plates 408 UHU.

9

The Designer

Dudley Hobbs was the chief designer at Bristol Cars from its inception in 1946 for three decades until 1976. Originally employed by the aeroplane company, he was one of those who transitioned to the car division after the war. He was responsible and involved in all models of the Bristol designed from the 400 to the 603. Having worked on wing aerodynamics, it is no coincidence that Hobbs's designs for the early Bristols were aerodynamic tour de forces. Coupled with the magnificently efficient 1,971 cc engine, the early Bristols were much sought after by drivers with spirited outlooks. All through the range of Bristol models it is possible to see the influence of the aircraft manufacturer in not only build quality but also in look and style. The 406 was perhaps less streamlined looking than its predecessors but it made up for this by an increased engine capacity to 2,261 cc, while of course by 1961 the 407 had an engine capacity of 5,130 cc. Even so the familial resemblance and hints of aircraft detail continued in the 408 and beyond on Hobbs's watch right up until the 603, which was produced from 1976 until 1982 and in which the lines drawn of the 407 model to that of the 411 are still visible.

Starting with the 400 model we have seen that there are not that many cosmetic changes from the BMW, which was its inspiration. Having said that Hobbs made a detailed analysis of the BMW 326 chassis, with each and every part converted to imperial measurement, creating an English car with appropriate screw threads and such like and with all English components utilised in the building of the Bristol. This made a much more refined and quieter car than its progenitor. Gradually though Hobbs had a freer hand with subsequent models, and we can see his aircraft industry background come to the fore in subtle details of his designs. For the six-cylinder models this included the radiator grille shape, which was reminiscent of an aeroplane nose cone dispensing with the BMW shape that had been retained on the 400 to 403. Other aircraft inspirations were the rear wing uplifts, perhaps best shown on the 404 and 405, and in particular the prototype 404, and which are still identifiable on the 408. If one were to place the 404 next to the largest aeroplane being developed by Bristol in the 1950s, the Brabazon Airliner, the styling cues immediately become apparent. The influence and knowledge gleaned from the production of aircraft is also apparent in the sports racing cars Bristol itself was running at the Le Mans 24 Hours in the 1950s. In the atrocious weather

An example of the four-door Bristol 405. Note the rear fins and radiator grille. (Mark Jansen/ Oldtimer Australia)

conditions experienced at the 1954 Le Mans endurance race the dynamic-looking Bristol 450 was the only full team of three cars to finish. In a full-page advertisement in *The Motor* on 23 June 1954 the company trumpeted the fact that it was 'The ONLY team to finish. The three Bristols ran consistently throughout, and covered the greatest distance ever for 2-litre cars'. The Bristols finished first, second and third in class and seventh, eight and ninth overall in a race in which some forty-one cars had to retire. That same advert in *The Motor* also made note of the fact that 'Powered by the famous Bristol 2-litre engine, the superbly elegant Type 403 and 404 Bristol cars are, too, distinguished by their brilliant performance and unfailing reliability.' The following year in the drastic 1955 race in which so many lives were lost when the Mercedes 300 SLR driven by Frenchman Pierre Levegh exploded into the crowd after going airborne off the back of Lance Macklin's Austin-Healey, which had swerved to avoid the rapidly slowing Jaguar D-Type piloted by eventual winner Mike Hawthorn, Bristol returned with open-topped cars. In this the final running of Le Mans after those eighty-four deaths the less extreme and futuristic looking Bristols, without the big rear fins again, finished in the same overall positions as in the preceding year. The difference was in the times though. As reported

The prototype 1953 Bristol 404 with its extraordinary and distinctive tail fin photographed at the 2022 Concorso d'Eleganza Villa d'Este. This car was originally owned by the company chairman, Sir George White. (James Nicholls)

The rear of the aeronautically inspired prototype 1953 Bristol 404. (James Nicholls)

by *The Autocar,* the fastest lap in 1954 had been 101.4 mph, which increased to 106.7 mph in 1955, while the top speeds recorded on the Mulsanne straight had been clocked at 132.9 mph in 1954 and 138.3 mph in 1955. Not a bad effort from 1,971 cc!

As his designs for Bristol evolved, Hobbs' influences appear to be much less BMW and now more Alfa Romeo, Carrozzeria Touring, and Ferrari after undertaking European visits to Milan, Geneva, Lugano and Paris. His design for the Bristol 406 marked the start of a big shift in the perception of the cars built by the marque. While the 406 still retained the Brabazon style front end, the rear, while still giving the nod to fins of its predecessors (especially on the prototype), is much more traditional, which did, however, provide a larger capacity for luggage. With the arrival of the 407, which was similar in shape to the 406 but with a revised front grille and the much bigger Chrysler engine, the die was cast for the magnificent 408 of which number 7001 was the first and foremost. The 408 is the apotheosis of the V8 cars and the first Bristol since the 404 to not carry the aero-engine-style front but rather now a more modern looking rectangular grille, low kick plates on the sides, with four headlamps for long touring and the flatter roof and bonnet lines. Yes, the 408 did look significantly different to its forebears but despite the radical change to the engine, it had been a process of evolution rather than revolution with the 408 able to trace its marque lineage back through its very successful forebears. And indeed, there were some very successful Bristols that followed in the footsteps of the 408. It is almost as if the Type 408 was the fulcrum of Bristol's achievements, right at the balancing point between Bristol's past and its future. The company had been in existence for just seventeen years

The Bristol 408-1-001. (James Nicholls)

Note the four headlights, rectangular grille, and low side kick plates of the Type 408. (James Nicholls)

when the 408 appeared in 1963 and would survive for over another half a century, but the launch of the 408 was a pivotal point of what went before, which can be described perhaps in one word – 'sporty' – and what came after, which could be luxurious. Having said that sportiness and luxuriousness tied together by the dignified use of the finest components and materials in the never-ending pursuit of quality can be seen throughout the line-up of all the Bristol Cars.

The Bristol 408 marked the end of an era and at the same time marked the dawn of a new age for the marque. Although the cars were still hand made to exacting standards, perhaps a little of the individuality was lost. No longer was it possible to order, inter alia, a Bristol Type 401 with a body by Pinin Farina or Touring Superleggera, a 406 by the Swiss house Beutler, or indeed the marvellous 406 and 407 of Zagato, or as Peter Sellers did a 407 with a convertible body by Viotto, the Torinese firm founded in 1921 by Vittorio Viotto and his partner Tolfo. Unfortunately, just twelve months after completing the Sellers car in 1963, a one-off that did not go into production due to 'overfull order books for saloons at that time' according to Bristol, Viotto closed its workshop doors in 1964. It was often Tony Crook, with his network of old racing and entrepreneurial contacts, who was the driving force behind these specials, but in the way of the motoring industry at that time the days of true coachbuilding were coming to an end. Having said that the

The Bristol 408. The end of an era. (James Nicholls)

408 was still coach-built in that the bodies were not made at Filton but 110 miles away in North West London.

In 1920 Hall, Lewis & Co. was established in Park Royal, in the London Borough of Brent. Much of its work comprised of making bodies for many Rolls-Royce chassis including a false cabriolet de ville on a Phantom II, along with coachwork for Minerva, Daimler and Lanchester, while it also made bodies for buses. Having gone bust in 1930, the company was relaunched as a bus manufacturer entitled Park Royal Coachworks Ltd. Apart from

The coach-built Bristol 406 by Beutler of Switzerland. (Bonhams)

The first of six coach-built Bristol 406s created by Zagato of Milan. (James Nicholls)

bus bodies after the war Park Royal was also responsible for fitting the bodies to Bristols including that of the new sixteen-gauge aluminium Type 408, with of course quality control carefully monitored by inspectors on permanent loan from Filton. Park Royal became part of the Leyland group before being closed down in 1980 as part of yet another rationalisation in the British motor industry.

A final note on the shape and style of the 408. While the genuine walnut woodwork, carpets and leather furnishings remained of the very highest quality along with the aluminium body and superior mechanics, are the rear tail lights not reminiscent of those from a Hillman Minx or Sunbeam Alpine from the same period? Still, no point reinventing the wheel unless one really must, and many an other bespoke car has picked up bits and pieces from the parts bin before and since!

In the same issue of *The Motor* magazine, in which the Bristol 408 appeared, 25 September 1963, was this image of the Sunbeam Alpine. Note the same tail lights used by both manufacturers. (James Nicholls)

10

What Came After

All stories have a beginning, a middle, and an end. Once upon a time there was an aircraft manufacturer who, of necessity and desire, decided to make cars. In the middle, cause and effect, came the Bristol 408. Sad to say, it did not all end up happily ever after. This is the story of the Bristol Car Company. We have looked at what went before the Bristol 408, but what came after? Well, initially, at the end of the two-year cycle 1963–65, the 408 Mk II, which was exactly the same as the Mk I but with the 318 Chrsyler engine as opposed to the 313, providing 5,211 cc, up from 5,130 cc, while the Torqueflite transmission housing was now made in aluminium. As we have seen, car 7001 acted somewhat as a mule for future development but the Type 409, produced between 1965 and 1967, and the Type 410 of 1967–69 were virtually identical to look at apart from minor changes to trim, though ZF power steering was added to the later 409s and on the 410. The 410 lost some of the Bristol idiosyncrasy by having its automatic gearbox control change from the push button on the dash to a traditional floor operated system. Between 1969 and 1975 followed five series of the Type 411, still looking very similar in style but with a bigger 6.2-litre engine providing rapid acceleration.

1975 saw a distinct shift in design style for Bristol and while the 603 continued the look, the 412 introduced that year was a convertible designed by Zagato. 1982 saw another departure from the Bristol norm as it tried to re-establish its image amid increasing competition. Numerical identification was dropped and the cars produced from 1982 onwards received names taken from the company's aircraft heritage. Somewhere, however, among the increased opulence and power it was still possible to recognise the familial resemblance of previous models in the Britannia, Brigand, and Blenhiem, while the Beaufighter was an updated targa version with an opening panel fixed front roof of the 412 model.

The final Bristol models from the first decade of the twenty-first century are something altogether different as Bristol went into the realm of the supercar territory with the two-seater Fighter with fashionable gull-wing doors and a V10 8-litre engine capable of over 200 mph. Very few were ever made from its introduction in 2004 before Bristol went into liquidation in 2011 and the Filton manufacturing facility closed down. Coming full circle Kamkorp, which also owned Frazer-Nash Research, a company like Bristol that

A fine example of the Bristol Type 409. Note the St George Flag below the Pegasus badge in the front wing is a later add on by its Italian Anglophile owner. (James Nicholls)

had undergone much since the two names had last worked together sixty years prior, purchased Bristol that year. It was announced that another new Bristol would emerge like a phoenix from the ashes and in 2016 in time for the 70th anniversary of the founding of the company, the Bristol Bullet broke cover and was displayed at Salon Privé. A two-seater sports car powered by a 4.8-litre BMW (what comes around goes around) V8 engine and sharing many build similarities to the Morgan Aero 8, it was a false dawn – just one Bullet was built and it was the Bristol name's last shot before on 5 March 2020 Bristol finally passed away.

The Bristol 408 was a remarkable motor car, hand built by a remarkable workforce for a remarkable motor car company. There had been many wonderful Bristols before its launch in 1963, and there were some excellent Bristols after the end of its run in 1965. However, it is surely the most Bristol of all Bristols and quite possibly the most desirable of all the models, apart perhaps from one or two built out of series, encapsulating as it does the unique nature and character and evolution of the machines built in Filton, the defining essence of all that is the very best of the archetypal, quintessential British motor car.

The Bristol Bullet was first seen at Salon Privé at Blenheim Palace in 2016. (James Nicholls)

Right: Morgan Aeromax, which sported the same BMW engine as the Bristol Bullet. (Courtesy of the owner).

Below: An overhead shot of the only Bristol Bullet built. Note the design references including rear fins to earlier models of the marque. (Bristol Cars Ltd)

Bibliography

Autocar Magazine (30 January 1948)
Autocar Magazine (25 September 1953)
Autocar Magazine (27 September 1963)
Autosport Magazine (16 October 1953)
Bristol Evening Post (27 April 1938)
Cars Illustrated Magazine (December 1964)
Motor Show Catalogue (October 1963)
Motorsport Magazine (April 2014)
The Motor Magazine (23 June 1954)
The Motor Magazine (23 September 1963)

Balfour, Christopher, *Bristol Cars, A Very British Story* (Yeovil: Haynes Publishing, 2009)
Big Chief I-Spy, *I-Spy Car Numbers* (London: The Dickens Press, 1968)
Clarke, R. M., *Bristol Cars 1946–2012 A Brooklands Portfolio* (Cobham: Brooklands Books, 2012)
D'Angelo, Sergio, *World Car Catalogue* (London: Iliffe Books, 1964)
Georgano, Nick, *The Beaulieu Encyclopedia of the Automobile, Coachbuilding* (Chicago: Fitzroy Dearborn Publishers, 2001)
George, Elizabeth, *The Inspector Lynley Mysteries* (1950s)
Guétat, Gérald, *Riva un sillage de rêves* (France: E-T-A-I, 2001)
Hobbs, John D., *Design and the Bristol Car* (Preston: Butterfield Press, 2022)
Pomeroy, Laurence, *The Grand Prix Car* (London: Motor Racing Publication, 1949)
Pritchard, A. G., *The Sporting Motorist* (October 1962)
Setright, L. J. K., *A Private Car, An Account of the Bristol* (England: Palawan Press, 1999)
Ward, Rod, *Fast Boats* (England: Zereo Publishing, 2008)
Wodehouse, P. G., *Aunts Aren't Gentlemen* (London: Barrie & Julian, October 1974)

www.bluemels.co.uk
www.bristolownersclubofaustralia.com.au
www.bristolownersheritagetrust.wordpress.com
www.connollybros.co.uk
www.k500.com
www.motors-mania.com